Financing Local Government

Commonwealth Secretariat
Local Government Reform Series

Nick Devas

with

Munawwar Alam, Simon Delay, Roger Oppong Koranteng and Pritha Venkatachalam

COMMONWEALTH SECRETARIAT

Commonwealth Secretariat
Marlborough House
Pall Mall
London SW1Y 5HX
United Kingdom

Published by the Commonwealth Secretariat
Edited and designed by Wayzgoose
Cover design by KC Gan Designs
Index by Indexing Specialists UK Ltd
Printed by The Charlesworth Group

Views and opinions expressed in this publication are the responsibility
of the authors and should in no way be attributed to the institutions to
which they are affiliated or to the Commonwealth Secretariat.

Wherever possible, the Commonwealth Secretariat uses paper sourced
from sustainable forests or from sources that minimise a destructive impact
on the environment.

Copies of this publication may be obtained from

The Publications Section
Commonwealth Secretariat
Marlborough House
Pall Mall
London SW1Y 5HX
United Kingdom
Tel: +44 (0)20 7747 6534
Fax: +44 (0)20 7839 9081
E-mail: publications@commonwealth.int
Web: www.thecommonwealth.org/publications

A catalogue record for this publication is available from the British Library.

ISBN: 978-0-85092-853-2 (paperback)
       978-1-84859-007-6 (downloadable e-book)

Foreword

Financing Local Government is the first title in the Commonwealth Secretariat's 'Local Government Reform' series. The Secretariat expects to publish a minimum of three titles in the series by 2010. The series editor and co-author is Dr Munawwar Alam, Adviser for Sub-National Government and Administration in the Secretariat's Governance and Institutional Development Division (GIDD).

The series will offer guidance on various aspects of local government reform to public sector policy-makers, senior managers at central and sub-national level, and students and researchers in public administration who have an interest in local government issues. It will feature contemporary thinking and summaries of international good practices from around the Commonwealth.

Decentralisation of government is now taking place in most Commonwealth developing countries. Local governments have assumed enhanced responsibilities for service delivery and the achievement of the Millennium Development Goals (MDGs), and there is a need to build capacity at local government level to keep pace with decentralisation. One of the crucial issues is the availability of adequate finances to satisfy public aspirations. Local leaders are concerned about the ability of government to mobilise and deploy financial resources effectively and efficiently.

This volume on municipal finance brings guidance and good practices to the attention of public sector executives who deal with local government finance. It is based upon the Executive Programme on Finance for Sub-national and Local Governments sponsored by the Commonwealth Fund for Technical Cooperation (CFTC). The programme has been delivered for three years in association with the University of Birmingham, UK; it exposes public officials to key issues and constraints on change in the area of municipal finance and outlines a strategic framework for capacity building. It sets out guidance on how to meet this challenge, supported by practical illustrations of Commonwealth innovations and international best practices.

The book explores methods of ensuring that fiscal decentralisation takes place at the same time as administrative decentralisation. It considers a range of available revenue sources, the design of systems of intergovernmental transfers and the rules needed to ensure that local governments manage their financial resources prudently. It also deals with more complex issues such as capital financing, municipal bonds, and accounting and auditing in local government. It highlights experiences in the UK and other Commonwealth countries, and presents a case study from Ghana.

The other book in this series, *Managing Change in Local Governance* (currently published in the 'Managing the Public Service – Strategies for Improvement' series), will be rebranded in subsequent editions. *Managing Change in Local Governance* is concerned with key issues in change management at sub-national level which follow on from decentralisation. It provides a useful reference tool for senior officers of national and sub-national governments who are poised to lead strategic change in local governance. GIDD will also publish case studies from Pakistan, Swaziland and The Gambia that will share cross-country experiences in local government reform.

I sincerely hope that this book will help policy-makers and managers entrusted with local government finances to create an effective and 'doable' financial framework for managing municipal budgets. Our aim is to strengthen local government reform strategies and processes, and enable Commonwealth governments to make more informed policy choices about decentralisation.

I am very grateful to Nick Devas, Director of the International Development Department at the University of Birmingham, for his collaboration and valuable contribution. Thanks are also due to the other contributors, Munawwar Alam, Simon Delay, Pritha Venkatachalam and Roger Oppong Koranteng, for sharing their expertise. GIDD is also grateful to Guy Bentham, in the Secretariat's Communications and Public Affairs Division, for assisting with the publication of this volume and for his helpful advice.

Jacqueline Wilson
Director
Governance and Institutional Development Division
Commonwealth Secretariat

Preface

The Commonwealth Secretariat Local Government Reform Series was launched by the Commonwealth Secretariat's Governance and Institutional Development Division (GIDD) to present contemporary trends, thinking and good practices in local government to local government practitioners, public sector policy-makers and all those working at sub-national level in the Commonwealth and internationally. As governments in developing countries decentralise, there is an urgent need for capacity building in local government.

This book aims to bring good practices in local government finance to the attention of public sector executives who deal with sub-national finance and of the local government finance community. The first book in the series, *Managing Change in Local Governance*,[1] concerns key issues that are central to managing change at the sub-national level in the context of emerging global trends in governance. Both books are essential reading for senior officers in local government and other officers in national and state governments who are leading strategic change in local governance in their countries. They are especially relevant for countries which have recently embarked upon the introduction of decentralising reforms.

The Commonwealth Secretariat's Governance and Institutional Development Division (GIDD) has developed an executive programme on finance for sub-national and local governments for Commonwealth member countries. So far, three sessions have been held in the UK. The programme incorporates practical examples and case studies, and field visits to UK local authorities to observe current practices. This book is based on the course material and modules developed for the programme by the University of Birmingham over the past three years.

GIDD is grateful to the Department of International Development at the University of Birmingham, and especially to Nick Devas, for their collaboration and the valuable contribution they have made to these books. It is hoped that policy-makers and practitioners will find the series a useful tool in guiding their local government reform strategies and processes in their own countries.

GIDD is also grateful to Guy Bentham, of the Secretariat's Communications and Public Affairs Division, for assisting in the preparation of this volume and for his helpful advice throughout the process of publication.

---

1 *Managing Change in Local Governance* was first published in the Commonwealth Secretariat's 'Managing the Public Service – Strategies for Improvement' series and will be rebranded in subsequent editions.

The Authors

Nick Devas is Director of the International Development Department, School of Public Policy at the University of Birmingham, UK.

Munawwar Alam is Adviser on Sub-National Government and Administration in the Governance and Institutional Development Division of the Commonwealth Secretariat.

Simon Delay is a consultant and lecturer at the School of Public Policy at the University of Birmingham, UK.

Roger Oppong Koranteng is senior lecturer at the Ghana Institute of Management and Public Administration, Accra, Ghana.

Pritha Venkatachalam is a financial specialist and senior consultant at Cambridge Economic Policy Associates, UK.

Contents

Financing Local Government

Munawwar Alam

Decentralisation is now taking place in most states, including Commonwealth member countries. This trend began in the 1980s and since then most countries have devolved some responsibilities to regional and local level. The move has been driven by the failure of the state to be sufficiently responsive to citizens' needs and regional differences and by the failure of centralised economic planning to deliver quality services to users at local level.

Irrespective of the reasons for decentralisation, reform initiatives have faced numerous challenges, especially in developing countries. These have involved the design of decentralised structures and the apportionment of resources and power between different tiers of sub-national government. Decentralisation has also placed increased responsibility for the delivery of public services and the achievement of the Millennium Development Goals on sub-national and local governments. This has especially been the case in federal systems, where regional and local governments have substantial responsibility for the provision of urban services and infrastructure. A critical determinant of the effective performance of sub-national and local governments is finance – their ability to mobilise financial resources and use them effectively. It follows that decentralisation requires the allocation of resources to sub-national and local governments so that they can finance their new role. This involves the assignment both of local government's own sources of revenue and of intergovernmental fiscal transfers.

The need for financial decentralisation

The decentralisation of administrative responsibilities and service delivery to lower tiers of governments without a corresponding reorganisation of finances is likely to be counter-productive. Fiscal decentralisation entails the assignment to sub-national or local governments of resources to finance the functions for which they are responsible. For there to be meaningful financial decentralisation, devolution of decision-making powers is also necessary. Own revenue sources include not only local taxes but revenues from charges, fees and other miscellaneous income sources. Intergovernmental fiscal transfers include the share of national tax revenues that is assigned to sub-national government and grants – both conditional and general.

In most countries, there are good reasons why the main sources of revenue accrue to central government; these include administrative practicality, economic efficiency and inter-regional equity. As a result, the own revenue sources assigned to local government are often quite limited, especially in rural areas. A system of intergovernmental transfers is therefore essential in order to ensure that local governments are able to carry out their responsibilities. A sound local financial system is critical to the integrity of the local public sector and for gaining the trust of citizens (Shah, 2007).

This book explores a variety of themes and topics relating to financial decentralisation. It starts by setting out the arguments for and against decentralisation and looking at its effects throughout the world. It asks what are the main sources of revenue for local governments and examines how local authorities administer their finances. It then moves on to explore more complex issues such as capital financing, municipal bonds and intergovernmental transfers. It discusses local government budgeting, accounting and auditing, as well as citizen participation and accountability at local level. Finally, the book highlights the experiences of particular countries, beginning with case studies of England and Ghana, and then looking briefly at other Commonwealth members.

In chapter 1, Nick Devas discusses how and why decentralisation is taking place in various parts of the world. He traces the trend towards centralisation in the period from the 1940s to the 1970s and towards decentralisation in the 1980s, and asks what were the drivers of reform. He makes it clear that there have been many different reasons for decentralisation and reviews the arguments for and against, backed by evidence taken from current literature.

Devas argues that fiscal decentralisation necessarily involves setting up systems to decide on the use of financial resources at sub-national level, and for monitoring and enforcement. This mechanism should contain the following important elements:

- Specification of local taxes

- The scope for local governments to levy fees and charges for locally provided services

- Regulations about the operations of local government-owned enterprises

- Regulations about borrowing by local governments

- Requirements regarding the execution of assigned functional responsibilities, including the level of discretion about the delivery of local services

- Specification of the use of intergovernmental transfers

- Systems of accounting and financial management

- External audit of the accounts of local government.

In chapter 2, Devas raises the fundamental issue of why local governments need resources in order to finance the services and activities for which they are responsible. Goods and services can be provided directly by local government or through contracting with or subsidising the private sector to provide them. Local government also has a variety of regulatory roles, such as building and development control and consumer protection, and these also have to be paid for.

Devas argues that local governments should be competent under law to levy a range of local taxes and charges, borne by residents of the jurisdiction, which will fund at least part of the cost of the services that benefit residents. This will also ensure that local decision-makers have a degree of discretion about the level of taxation. However, in reality most local governments only partially meet local expenditure needs from local sources. There are complex issues of equity and efficiency here, and these are discussed in the chapter. On the issue of taxation and equity, Caulfield (1997) argues that the real issue is whether improvements in local finances, including the taxation system, can strengthen local economies and reduce inequality, thereby reducing threats to social cohesion in urban areas.

In light of the fact that in most countries local governments are chronically short of resources, there is a need to examine options on how to fill this gap. Devas suggests various ways of doing this, including control of expenditure, exploiting the tax base and improving revenue collection, charging for services, increasing the transfer of funds from central government and borrowing. The chapter throws light on several related issues which no local government can afford to ignore in its efforts to increase local revenue, such as the cost of collection, equity and enforcement. It also deals with various forms of local taxation. Devas argues that the most suitable local taxes are those where the tax base is wholly confined within a jurisdiction, is immobile and is similar to that in other jurisdictions. This is why property taxes are the commonest form of local taxation around the world. In the OECD countries, there are two main sources of local revenue – income tax and property tax. English-speaking countries tend to depend on the latter (Caulfield, 1997); the chapter also discusses their relative merits.

Chapter 3 deals with local revenue administration. Devas argues that improving tax administration is as important as the reform of tax policy. The chapter deals with all stages of local revenue administration, including tariff setting, taxpayer identification, tax collection, enforcement, accounting for taxes collected, and reporting on and monitoring results. It goes on to discuss performance indicators for revenue administration, for example tax effort, effectiveness and efficiency.

Devas suggests some effective revenue administration practices, such as taxpayer identification, better records management and giving minimum discretion to assessors. He also argues for compartmentalisation of the functions of assessment and collection, and the rotation of staff on a regular basis. Where possible, local taxes and charges should be designed to ensure that payment is made in full at the earliest date – for example, for water and electricity charges. The whole system will be thwarted if there are not adequate checks and controls. In particular, the system of recording assessments and payment should be straightforward and amenable to checking.

Raising the public's consciousness of the importance of taxation is vital to the sustainability of the system. There is an important educational task to be done in making the public aware of the need to pay their taxes promptly. This can best be done by providing proper information on how revenues are used. Soliciting the help of community leaders in presenting the information and exhorting the community to pay its taxes may have some positive results, particularly if community leaders feel they have an input about how the resources are to be used, and if they are seen to directly benefit the local community.

Chapter 4 deals with financing capital investment. Large-scale local governments require big investments in municipal infrastructure to create or improve local services. There are several ways of financing capital expenditure, such as borrowing from central government, raising loans from international agencies, for example the World Bank, borrowing from a central credit institution or facility for local authorities, as well as direct borrowing from the public or the money market, for example by issuing local authority bonds. Devas makes a lucid assessment of the pros and cons of local government borrowing. Borrowing by sub-national entities is a complex issue which can sometimes have serious impact on macroeconomic management. While presenting the arguments for and against borrowing, the author considers complex economic issues such as inflation and economic growth, and argues for more stringent technical and financial scrutiny of projects that are to be financed from loans as compared with those financed from the recurrent budget. The chapter also deals with alternative ways in which capital investments by local governments can be financed, including public-private partnerships.

Typically, cities in emerging market countries have growing urban populations, and service capabilities that are unable to keep pace with rising demand. Further, the increasing devolution of functions to municipal level is often incommensurate with the fiscal capabilities granted to the city. In the face of these constraints, most national and local governments are seeking alternative forms of market-based financing to supplement their revenue sources, and are trying to attract private sector participation in the delivery of services. While some municipalities have the institutional and financial strength to access market-based financing directly, others are establishing special purpose funds or facilities to attract private financing for infrastructure services.

In this context, chapter 5 sets out international experiences of accessing credit and capital markets to finance infrastructure and presents a case study of the Tamil Nadu Urban Development Fund (TNUDF) in South India. Pritha Venkatachalam argues that while the TNUDF pioneered several innovative approaches to urban infrastructure financing through the issue of bonds, there has been limited thrust on developing the demand-side capabilities of local government in preparing bankable projects. In order to develop long-term sustainable access to capital markets as a source of finance for municipal infrastructure, projects need to be commercially viable and close to operational readiness in order to pay back the borrowed funds. A successful innovation in Tamil Nadu was 'pooled financing'. Thirteen small municipalities aggregated their water and sanitation requirements and raised about Rs 300 million through a pooled bond issue. The layered structure of credit enhancements and the principle of credit aggregation boosted investor confidence in subscribing to these bonds and enabled local bodies to access market finance at competitive interest rates.

The chapter concludes that financial market innovations and reforms should be accompanied by stronger project preparation and development capability of local governments. This is essential to increase creditworthy investment opportunities for market-based financing and develop commercial financing as a long-term alternative to the traditional revenue sources of local governments.

Chapter 6 discusses the crucial issue of intergovernmental fiscal transfers. It covers the full range of transfers from central government to sub-national and local governments, including:

- Tax/revenue sharing

- General (block) grants

- Specific grants

- Deficit grants

- Capitalisation grants

- Subsidised loans.

The design of the intergovernmental transfer system is extremely important, as is the General Budgetary Support (GBS) mechanism. This is absolutely critical in determining the extent to which local government can benefit from new approaches to aid. Amis (2007) recommends that ministries of local government and local governments should be considered as a key stakeholders in the GBS and other central policy-making activities.

The chapter deals with the criteria for evaluating intergovernmental transfer systems: adequacy, elasticity and stability, inter-regional equity, economic efficiency and simplicity. As there is always tension between central and local government, central-local transfers raise complex issues. Another facet of this relationship is that financial flows from central government do not necessarily imply the political subjugation of the sub-national entity. There are examples of local governments that receive a large proportion of their revenues from the centre without any diminution of their local discretion (for example in the Netherlands); in other countries, local governments are tightly controlled by the centre, even where they do not receive significant funds (for example in Kenya). Devas gives a comprehensive account of these issues and argues that the impact of the transfer system on local governments should be regularly monitored, so that undesirable results can be corrected. However, the system also requires stability – frequent changes to the formula destabilise decentralised service provision.

Chapter 7 deals with budgeting and expenditure management. It begins with the key roles played by financial planning and budgeting and recurrent and capital budgets, and then discusses the sub-national government budget preparation process. The chapter stresses that it is important that the estimates prepared by local government departments are based on adequate guidance from the municipal finance department on resource limits, policy priorities, etc. This enables services managers to plan realistically within the available resources. In the absence of such guidance, spending departments are likely to bid high ('pad their bids') in the expectation of cuts, obliging the central finance department to make arbitrary decisions about cuts in budget proposals later in the process. There are also strategic choices which need to be made by elected representatives through a proper policy process based on agreed objectives and strategies.

Debate about the extent and level of state involvement in the economy and its impact on corruption continues in the literature (Becker, 1994). Galtung (1998) has argued that there is a correlation and puts forward the thesis that the distribution of power is more important than the extent of government activity. Decentralised financial management requires the manager to deliver specified service levels and performance and potentially puts more public resources at risk, in the sense that more resources are handled at locations remote from direct central control, with more people having an influence on how the resources are used. Therefore, decentralisation may disperse corruption more widely, although it may not increase the overall level – indeed, it may help to curb corruption through greater accountability. This chapter also draws attention to the reforms to financial management employed in many countries, such as simplifying accounting systems, computerisation of revenue collection and paying grants directly from the Ministry of Finance to the bank account of the sub-national government. Devas argues that decentralisation involves a shift from a direct role played by central government in service delivery to one of enabling and monitoring the work of local governments. Decentralisation requires that central government pays agreed grants and revenue shares on time, and that it seeks to reinforce good practice at local level.

The cost of services provided by local governments is measured in terms of money, because governments have to buy from the same markets as other businesses; but the effect of financing governments by taxation is that beneficiaries do not express their satisfaction in money terms (Jones, 2007). In chapter 8, Simon Delay argues that effective systems of accounting are essential, not only to provide managers in local government with the financial information they need to manage their services, but also to account to citizens and taxpayers for the use of public resources. However, Delay maintains that conventional accounting is good at identifying costs, but poor at identifying performance. Therefore, accounting as a tool needs to be combined with other approaches in order to assess the performance of a public body such as a local government.

Delay also argues that monitoring budgets is essential not only to avoid overspending, but also to avoid underspending that might threaten performance in service delivery. However, budget monitoring provides only a limited insight into overall performance. Delay also notes how government spending is monitored in the UK, where there are two principal governmental external audit bodies: the National Audit Office, which is responsible for auditing central government; and the Audit Commission, which audits local government.

Delay points out that there is a fine line between over-regulation and local autonomy. He argues that perhaps a natural consequence of increased devolution and local autonomy is the lack of trust (much of which may be justified) on the part of central government towards local government. There is therefore often a danger of over-regulation. Moreover, we should not ignore the fact that audit and inspection have heavy compliance costs, putting a strain on limited capacity and possibly encouraging rent-seeking behaviour by inspectors and auditors. Over-regulation and excessive inspection and audit can discourage local initiative and risk-taking.

Competition between audit and inspection agencies may be healthy, but it may also lead to turf wars. Efforts at scrutiny need to be co-ordinated to ensure greatest benefit. There are also important issues relating to who scrutinises the scrutineers and who guards the guardians.

International experience indicates that efficient and accountable local governments are those where the people who make the spending decisions, those who enjoy the benefits and those who pay the taxes are the same (Slack, 2006). In chapter 9, Devas broadly deals with citizens' participation and local government accountability. In most contemporary societies, citizens elect councillors who make decisions about local services and levy local taxes to pay for those services. The citizen's only role is to vote in elections every four years or so and pay their local taxes. This is the traditional view of local government, which is being increasingly challenged. Citizens now expect to have a greater say in the running of the services that affect them. They are dissatisfied by the lack of accountability of those they have elected for the taxes they have levied and other resources they have used. In many countries, they are concerned about the level of corruption in local government. Devas argues that councillors are able to make decisions without any democratic participation or accountability to citizens from one election to the next. Local political processes are often dominated by local elites, who may rely on patronage networks to ensure their re-election. Little information is available on which to judge the performance of those who have been elected. In view of these constraints, Devas suggests that for decisions on more specific issues, other mechanisms of participation are needed. He cites some participatory mechanisms, but hints that it is important to be realistic about what can be achieved within any particular situation.

Devas also indicates that participatory processes do not necessarily help the poor, who lack the time, resources and education to participate effectively. What matters is the attitude and commitment of the politicians and officials involved in the process.

In the context of accountability at local level, civil society is significant. However, one should not be oblivious of the fact that civil society is also riddled with divisions along racial, ethnic, religious and political lines and reflects various conflicts of interest.

Chapters 10 to 12 present country case studies. Chapter 10 discusses an example from a developed Commonwealth country – local government in England. This is followed in chapter 11 by a detailed case study of a developing country, Ghana. Finally, chapter 12 reviews current practices in selected Commonwealth countries which are at different stages of development and looks at some common denominators.

Chapter 10 focuses on local government and local government finance in England. (Scotland, Wales and Northern Ireland have slightly different systems.) It summarises the evolution of English local government and describes its current structure. The chapter also covers the functions of local government and their division between two tiers. In some places, unitary authorities are responsible for all aspects of local government. However in London, the Greater London Authority has powers in relation to strategic planning and transportation, with the remaining functions being carried out by the London boroughs. Some important functions commonly assigned to local government are not local government functions in England: for example, health (a central government function devolved through the National Health Service), social welfare payments (handled by the central government's Benefits Agency) and utilities such as water, sewerage, electricity, gas and telecommunications (all now run by privatised companies). The police service, which was formerly a local government function (except in London), is now the responsibility of regional police authorities which consist of representatives of both central and local government. The chapter also gives a full picture of local government finance in England, including the council tax, transfers from central government, capital financing, financial management and auditing.

In chapter 11, Dr Oppong Koranteng presents a case study of Ghana. He analyses how politics have facilitated or constrained fiscal decentralisation by examining the response to the country's fiscal decentralisation policies. The chapter also looks at how politics within the various policy networks affects fiscal decentralisation, and shows how the various stakeholders have different interests and resources, which influence the implementation of fiscal decentralisation policies.

The analysis suggests that resistance to the implementation of fiscal decentralisation has come from the central government's Ministry of Finance. The implementation of centralisation is technically and administratively complex in situations where there is low public participation and visibility. It is apparent from the case study that reactions to fiscal decentralisation have been generated in the bureaucratic arena, which has a low political stake in reform.

The Commonwealth is extremely diverse – and so is the way in which local governance is conducted in member countries. Though decentralisation is taking place in many Commonwealth countries, there are wide variations in the pace of reform. The reasons behind decentralisation and local government reform also differ from country to country. The final chapter presents contrasting perspectives on systems of local government finance in the many Commonwealth countries that have participated in the Secretariat's flagship programme over the last three years. In order to cover the main areas and current practices, the chapter focuses on the following issues:

- External control of local finances by the central or state/provincial government ministry, e.g. approval of the budget, taxes and loans;

- Current annual taxation capacity;

- Potential for improvement of revenue mobilisation;

- Ratio of taxes collected to taxes due;

- Generation of revenue from service charges;

- Central-local financial relations – the kind and extent of intergovernmental transfers;

- Ability to access capital markets;

- Local government bonds as a mechanism for raising capital;

- Audit of local government accounts;

- E-governance processes, e.g. for payment of taxes, dues and licence fees, and for making complaints;

- How budgeting can be made more open to public influence.

The chapter includes short case studies of Malaysia, Jamaica, Sierra Leone, Malta, Mauritius, Nigeria and Sri Lanka.

The issue of finance cannot be considered independently of the purposes that local government is intended to serve. In order to meet the challenges of the twenty-first century, local governments need to be given power and resources that are commensurate with their changing responsibilities. The need for reform is clear. However, financial decentralisation raises complex issues, and it is these that are the theme of this book.

References and further reading

Amis, P. (2007). 'Financing Decentralisation and Local Government to Meet the MDGs', Paper prepared for Commonwealth Local Government Forum and Com-Habitat, Commonwealth Finance Ministers Meeting, Guyana, October.

Becker, G. (1994). 'To root out corruption, boot out big government', *Business Week*, 31 January.

Blore, I., Devas, N. and Slater, R. (2004). *Municipalities and Finance*. London: Earthscan.

Caulfield, J. (1997). 'Taxation and Equities Within Metropolitan Areas', Paper presented to OECD Workshop on Governing Metropolitan Areas. Paris: OECD, June.

Galtung, F. (1998). 'Criteria for Sustainable Corruption Control', in Robinson, M. (ed.), *Corruption and Development*. London: Frank Cass, pp. 105–28.

Jones, R. (2007). 'Financial Accounting and Reporting', in Shah, A. (ed.), *Local Public Financial Management*. Washington, DC: World Bank.

Shah, A. (ed.) (2007). *Local Public Financial Management*. Washington, DC: World Bank, p. 1.

Slack, E. (2006). *Dialogues*. Toronto: Canada West Foundation.

CHAPTER ONE

Decentralisation and the Implications for Local Government Finance

Nick Devas

Decentralisation: A global trend

Decentralisation is not new. Almost every country in the world (except some very small states) has some form of sub-national government structure, whether to maintain control or to deliver public services across the country, or both. Sub-national structures range from elected state, provincial, municipal or local governments with high degrees of autonomy, to local agents of the central state with minimal discretion – with numerous variations in-between.

Within the Commonwealth, the local government system varies widely, a reflection of the Commonwealth's diverse nature. Variations arise in terms of constitutional protection for local governments (about 25 countries), number of tiers, gender participation, financial autonomy and intergovernmental transfers. Many Commonwealth countries do not have a local government system *per se*, while in others local governments have limited functions and autonomy.

As decentralisation is a global trend, Commonwealth countries are at different stages of reform; the pace of implementation also varies. In low- and middle-income Commonwealth members, decentralisation is closely linked to the new global agenda for poverty reduction and attainment of the Millennium Development Goals. In high-income member nations, the pressure comes from the need to squeeze greater 'value for money' from existing fiscal revenue and central government transfers. At the same time, in many countries there has been new thinking about shifting away from the direct provision of services by government to more indirect approaches in partnership with the private sector (e.g. public-privatisation partnership legislation in Fiji Islands) and community based organisations (e.g. citizen community boards in Pakistan).

The decentralisation debate addresses the central problem of public administration – that of 'delegated discretion' (Fukuyama, 2004). The centralisation/decentralisation debate tends to be cyclical. Central governments have a natural tendency to centralise, until some countervailing pressure forces decentralisation. Colonial governments often used decentralised government arrangements as a way of extending their control, e.g. through 'indirect rule' or as providing 'education for democracy' in the run-up to independence (Mawhood, 1993; Olowu and Wunsch, 2004). From the 1940s to the

1970s there was a centralising tendency in much of the world: under communism in central and eastern Europe, the Soviet Union and China; in newly independent countries, where governments sought to consolidate their authority; and as a result of attempts at central economic planning in much of the developing world.

Since the 1980s, there has been a strong tendency to devolve functions, with most countries adopting some form of decentralisation. This has been driven by:

- The failure of the central state to be sufficiently responsive to citizen needs and regional differences;

- The failure of centralised economic planning to deliver results;

- Democratisation in large parts of the world, with demands from local communities to control their own resources in accordance with local needs and priorities;

- The rise of secessionist movements demanding autonomy from the centre;

- Urbanisation and the growth of large, complex cities, necessitating more responsive systems of city governance;

- Budget problems of national governments, for which decentralisation of responsibilities is often seen (erroneously) as a solution;

- Donor pressures on governments to decentralise as a way of improving service delivery at the periphery, and of getting around obstructions at the centre.

Often, adverse or limited results from earlier attempts result in renewed centralisation, only to be followed by further attempts at decentralisation when the shortcomings of excessive centralisation become evident once more.

Within Europe, the basic treaties of the European Union specify subsidiarity as a principle – that is, that government functions should be carried out at the lowest level that can perform those functions effectively and efficiently.

In practice, decentralisation (or its reverse) is not a once-for-all reform, but rather a continuous process of change in response to particular circumstances and drivers.

The case for decentralisation

The arguments for decentralisation essentially fall into three overlapping groups: administrative, political and economic.

Administrative arguments

It is simply not possible to make every decision about every part of a country from the centre. The centre lacks detailed knowledge about local needs and conditions. Since services have to be delivered at the local level, at least some decisions have to be made locally. This is similar to the way in which commercial organisations decentralise certain decisions to local managers. The larger and more diverse the country, the greater is the administrative need to decentralise.

Political arguments

Democratic governance implies that citizens exercise choice about how resources are used and services delivered in their communities. Local self-government increases opportunities for participation and accountability, thereby deepening democracy and increasing democratic legitimacy. This is especially so where a country's population is diverse, and needs and preferences vary between regions. In principle, decentralisation can increase opportunities for participation and access to decision-making by otherwise excluded groups, as well as increasing accountability, through proximity of decision-makers to citizens. It also provides a means of accommodating the legitimate aspirations of regionally-based ethnic groups for a degree of autonomy.

Economic arguments

Decentralisation, it is argued, can bring about an improved allocation of resources, as decisions about resource use better reflect the needs, priorities and willingness to pay of local citizens. As a result, service delivery should improve. So should cost recovery and resource mobilisation, as local charge and taxpayers will be more willing to pay for services that benefit them (although the evidence on the last point seems quite weak).

> ... the power over the production and delivery of goods and services should be rendered to the lowest unit capable of capturing the associated costs and benefits.
>
> World Bank, *World Development Report 1997*, p. 120

Fiscal federalism: The classic theoretical case for decentralisation is often referred to as fiscal federalism (Oates, 1972). This argues that, since the efficient scale of production for most public goods is smaller than the national level, economic benefits will be maximised where decisions about those public goods are made within the jurisdiction which relates to the scale of production of those public goods, so as to reflect differing preference patterns. Under such an arrangement, costs and benefits can be internalised – that is, the costs and benefits of a service fall on those within that jurisdiction who make the decisions. The problem is that public goods have differing spatial characteristics and economies of scale, so that different 'local governments' would be required for each service. Since that is generally impractical, a compromise has to be found in terms of the optimum size for a multi-purpose local government (although in many countries there are special-purpose authorities, for example school boards and police districts in the USA).

Public choice: Tiebout (1956), in his application of public choice theory to decision-making in local government, argues that citizens will vote for a combination of taxes and benefits that best suit their interests ('voice'), and/or will relocate to the jurisdiction which offers the best combination of services and taxes ('exit'). Although there are examples that support this 'exit' model (e.g. firms and rich residents relocating out of New York City), this theory makes unrealistic assumptions about citizens' ability and willingness to relocate, as well as about the information available to them, particularly in developing countries.

Variety, experiment and competition: A further economic argument for decentralisation is that it allows a variety of experiments and initiatives that can, through comparison and learning, improve the overall performance of the system. Furthermore, competition between jurisdictions may enhance overall performance of the governmental system. By contrast, centralised systems tend to standardise and fossilise. But this assumes that experimentation, innovation and competition are possible within the system, and that there are mechanisms for mutual learning. These are relatively rare in developing countries.

Poverty reduction and gender equality: It is often argued that decentralisation can contribute to poverty reduction by bringing decision-making closer to where the poor live, increasing the voice of and accountability to the poor, and by more accurate targeting of social spending. It could bring positive results if the decentralised system incorporates mechanisms to redistribute resources between regions or local governments. However, where poverty arises from inequalities within the region or local government, decentralisation could even worsen the plight of the poor as a result of local elite capture. The evidence on the impact of decentralisation on poverty is very mixed (Jütting et al., 2004). A general conclusion is that decentralisation alone is unlikely to have a positive effect on poverty and inequality unless there are particular initiatives to address these issues. More specifically, unless decentralised government systems make provision to ensure the representation and voice of women, decentralisation is unlikely to bring about greater gender equality.

The arguments against decentralisation

The following are common arguments against decentralisation:

a) *Fragile national unity*, particularly in newly independent nations, and the perception that decentralisation could result in fragmentation and reinforce ethnic divisions. In practice, however, while tight central control in a diverse nation may work for a while, it can often collapse dramatically (e.g. USSR, Indonesia). By contrast, decentralisation may provide a safety valve for those seeking a degree of autonomy.

b) *Increased inter-regional inequality:* Since some regions have greater resources and greater economic potential, according regions greater autonomy may increase inequality across the country. Although there are ways of combating this, through intergovernmental fiscal transfers (see chapter 6) and redirecting investment, the evidence from many countries (for example China, Mexico, Indonesia and, to a lesser extent, India) is that decentralisation has, in practice, increased inter-regional inequality (Rodríguez-Pose and Gill, 2004).

c) *Decentralisation is unnecessary* (in the sense of devolution) because local needs and priorities can be determined by central officials placed in the regions (i.e. deconcentration) without the need for devolution of political power. It is often argued that such 'benign centralism' may do more to achieve local development (as evidenced in several countries in east and south-east Asia) than factious local democracy. But this approach leaves open issues of citizen voice and local accountability for decisions.

d) *Cost and inefficiency:* Decentralisation can add to the costs of public administration by increasing the numbers of elected representatives (who generally require some remuneration) and local officials. However, these costs may be necessary if services are to be brought to the local level and decisions made in a participatory and accountable manner. Decentralisation may also result in inefficiency, where services are provided by each small community at below the efficient scale of operation (a major issue in central and eastern Europe post-1990). This problem can be overcome (as in France) by joint operation between local governments and/or contracting services from other local governments or private suppliers (i.e. making a distinction between providing a service and producing it – it is the latter, not the former, that requires economies of scale).

e) *Lack of capacity* at the local level, whether through lack of technical or managerial skills or low calibre of staff. This is often a serious issue, but tends to become self-fulfilling where it is used as the reason for not decentralising activities, since the result is that there is no incentive for skilled people to stay at the local level. The problem can be addressed (to some extent) by training and/or secondment of staff from higher tier(s) of government.

f) *Lack of financial resources* at the local level, since local tax bases are small (particularly in rural areas). However, this is not a reason for not decentralising – rather, the intergovernmental fiscal system needs to be designed so that the distribution of functions between levels of government is matched by fiscal resource transfers (see chapter 6).

g) *Increased fiduciary risks and corruption:* Since more resources are handled further from the centre, where financial controls are generally weaker, there are increased fiduciary risks. Corruption may also be more serious at the local level because of the proximity of officials and politicians to clients and contractors. However, the same proximity, to citizens and voters, may also help to increase accountability. There is ongoing debate about whether decentralisation makes the problems of corruption better or worse, or just disperses the problem more widely (Fjeldstad, 2004).

h) **Threats to macroeconomic management and stability:** Decentralisation may reduce the room for manoeuvre for national governments in managing the economy, and in extreme cases can be destabilising (Prud'homme, 1995; World Bank, 1997: 125; Tanzi, 2000). This can occur where large areas of taxation are assigned to, or shared with, local governments without matching increases in their functions, where local governments are free to borrow without proper limits or where they incur substantial budget deficits. These have been significant problems in a number of Latin American countries, and to a lesser extent in China, but in most other developing countries, the local government sector is too small or too highly controlled by the centre, or both, to have any serious impact on national economic management. Prudential rules about borrowing and deficits can largely obviate the problem. The perception that local government borrowing is generally irresponsible is changing, and countries such as India have started institutionalising borrowing from the private sector for municipal infrastructure financing (see chapter 4).

i) **Domination by local elites** and traditional authority structures may be to the disadvantage or exclusion of the poor. It is argued (Manor, 1999) that local elites are generally less favourable to the poor than central government elites. However, whether the poor are more disadvantaged or excluded in a decentralised system than in a centralised one is still a matter of debate. Much depends on the local and national political processes, and the opportunities for the voice of and accountability to different groups, in the particular country.

j) **Resistance from central government officials:** In practice, the main resistance to decentralisation is likely to come from central government politicians and civil servants, who perceive that their power is being eroded. Even when they officially endorse decentralisation, their actions may impede or undermine the process.

What is the evidence?

A number of recent studies have shed light on the effects of decentralisation.

Blair's (2000) study of democratic local governance in six countries showed that in most cases there had been benefits in terms of extending participation and accountability, but that there had been little impact on inequality or poverty. The impact on participation and accountability depended on the range of mechanisms adopted.

Crook and Manor's (1998) study of four countries (Karnataka in India, Bangladesh, Côte d'Ivoire and Ghana) found mixed results:

• Performance in terms of output of public services improved in most cases, but strongly only in Karnataka;

- Indicators of responsiveness and citizen satisfaction ranged from good in Karnataka to poor in Ghana;

- Certain poor groups may benefit from decentralisation but others are unlikely to;

- It is the combination of various factors (notably, political commitment, resources, popular participation and mechanisms of accountability) that account for whether or not decentralisation is effective.

In their cross-country analysis of studies of the impact of decentralisation on poverty-alleviation, Crook and Sverrisson (2001) found that:

- Decentralisation is unlikely to increase pro-poor performance except where this is driven by central (or state level) government (e.g. in West Bengal and in some Brazilian states);

- There is a common pattern of 'elite capture' of elected local governments, often encouraged from the centre;

- Accountability is critical: top-down, unaccountable decentralisation processes have not helped the poor (e.g. Ghana, Côte d'Ivoire, Bangladesh, Kenya, Nigeria and Mexico);

- Poverty reduction requires effective arrangements for allocating both financial and administrative resources that ensure the intended use of transferred resources and the capacity to implement programmes;

- Outcomes depend on the length of time which the decentralised system has been in operation (e.g. West Bengal compared to most other places);

Schneider's (2003) statistical study of 108 countries found:

- That deconcentrated governmental systems spend more on social services, while politically devolved governmental systems spend less on these;

- No correlation between fiscal decentralisation and pro-poor expenditure;

- That the interests of the poor are best served by a combination of political central-isation and administrative deconcentration.

By contrast, Von Braun and Grote's (2000) comparison of human development indica-tors with the extent of political decentralisation concludes that decentralisation can be beneficial to the poor under the right circumstances, and that it is political rather than administrative decentralisation that makes the greatest difference. This is because of the greater scope for the poor both to hold elected officials accountable and to influ-ence public spending decisions when they are concentrated in certain jurisdictions.

Overall, the evidence on decentralisation is mixed and contested. In a number of coun-tries (Indonesia, Philippines) problems arising from rapid and substantial decentralisation have led to calls for a degree of recentralisation. These may have the support of powerful interests. Nevertheless, there is a general point that can be made. Local services, on which the poor depend, have to be delivered 'out there', so that some form of decentralisation is necessary. What matters, then, is how the system is designed and the mechanisms that are incorporated to ensure 'voice' and accountability.

Forms and principles of decentralisation

In the literature and in common usage, terms are not always used precisely. Some use the term decentralisation to refer to any shift away from the centre, whether managerial/administrative (e.g. within a company or organisation), political, spatial or fiscal. Here we make a basic distinction between deconcentration and devolution.

- *Deconcentration* (sometimes also referred to as administrative or management decentralisation): responsibilities are assigned to agents of the central government.

- *Devolution* (also referred to as political decentralisation or democratic decentralisation): responsibilities and authority assigned to elected bodies with some degree of local autonomy.

Deconcentration is concerned mainly with the administrative rationale for decentralising and to some extent with the economic arguments, whereas devolution to elected local bodies is concerned with the political as well as the economic (and administrative) arguments.

The distinction is not always clear-cut. Deconcentrated units may well have considerable discretion about how to operate and may have resources under their control (e.g. local managers in the UK's National Health Service). Meanwhile, devolved local governments may be tightly controlled by the centre, with limited discretion over resource use. But the difference in principle is that the former are answerable only to their parent ministry or agency, whereas the latter are primarily answerable to the local electorate (although there will also be an upward accountability to central government).

In the past, some governments (e.g. Tanzania, Kenya) have used the term decentralisation to refer to a process of shifting power to deconcentrated agents of central government (e.g. district commissioners), while at the same time reducing the role of elected local governments.

Two further forms of decentralisation are often mentioned, although they do not really affect the basic distinction drawn here. One is delegation, where a government agency or a sub-national government carries out a particular function on behalf of central government in return for a payment. This can take place within either a deconcentrated or devolved system.

The other is fiscal decentralisation, which is the transfer of fiscal resources and decision-making power to the sub-national level, usually to an elected regional or local government. However, fiscal decentralisation does not usually exist on its own: it requires devolution of decision-making power in order to be meaningful, while devolution of decision-making power requires fiscal decentralisation in order to be meaningful. Fiscal decentralisation will be discussed further below, as well as in subsequent chapters.

Requirements for effective decentralised (devolved) government: Decentralisation in the form of devolution requires a system of local government that has:

- Boundaries, powers and functions defined in law;

- A separate legal identity with perpetual succession, able to buy, sell and hold property, and with its own budget and bank account;

- An elected decision-making body, although some members may be appointed;

- Significant discretion over local expenditures;

- Some independent source(s) of finance over which it has some discretion in setting the level and using the receipts;

- Its own staff (although they may belong to a unified national cadre and some may be seconded from central government).

Relationships between deconcentrated and devolved authorities: In most systems, a key issue is the relationship between the devolved local governments and the deconcentrated agents of the state (such as prefects, district commissioners, collectors, intendente and the local offices of central ministries). This concerns:

- Territorial authority (who is 'in charge'?)

- Division of functions (who does what?)

- Representation (who represents the local population?)

- Supervision and control (who supervises whom?).

In some countries, there are two parallel systems (e.g. prefect or district commissioner and commune or local government), often with considerable friction between the two. In other countries (e.g. Indonesia), the two are combined, so that a provincial governor is both the head of the provincial government and the representative of central government locally.

Fiscal decentralisation

Decentralisation – at least in the sense of devolution to elected local governments – requires fiscal decentralisation. Fiscal decentralisation is the assignment to subnational or local governments of resources to finance the functions that have been assigned to them. This involves the assignment of both local own revenue sources and intergovernmental fiscal transfers.

Local own revenue sources include not only local taxes, but also revenues from charges and fees, from local owned enterprises and other miscellaneous income sources. These will be discussed in more detail in chapter 2. Intergovernmental fiscal transfers include shares of revenues from national taxes that are assigned to sub-national or local government, and grants, both conditional grants and general or block grants. These will be discussed in more detail in chapter 6.

Fiscal decentralisation involves the design of an overall intergovernmental fiscal system that achieves both vertical and horizontal balance:

- Vertical balance between the functions assigned to each level of government and the resources assigned;

- Horizontal balance between the expenditure needs and resource capacity of each unit at the same level (i.e. between local governments at the same level in a multi-tier system).

In most systems, the main revenue sources are assigned to central government, for good reasons of administrative practicality, economic efficiency and inter-regional equity. As a result, the local own revenue sources assigned to local government are often quite limited, and in rural areas may yield very little revenue indeed. Therefore, a system of intergovernmental transfers is essential in order to ensure that local governments can carry out the responsibilities assigned to them. The design of such systems will be discussed further in chapter 6.

Fiscal decentralisation also involves a set of rules about the use of financial resources at sub-national level, and systems for monitoring and enforcing those rules. These rules may relate to:

- The specification of local taxes, including the system of assessment;

- The scope for local governments to levy fees and charges for locally provided services;

- Regulations about the operations of local government-owned enterprises;

- Regulations about borrowing by local governments;

- Requirements regarding the execution of assigned functional responsibilities, including the level of discretion about the delivery of local services;

- Specification of the use of intergovernmental transfers;

- The form of the local expenditure plans and budgets, including approval of development plans and annual budgets;

- Systems of accounting and financial management;

- External audit of the accounts of local government.

Financing Local Government

Central government's ability to monitor and enforce these regulations is, however, often constrained by:

- Limited knowledge at the centre about what is actually happening at the local level;

- Lack of staff at the centre to monitor and control the activities of numerous local governments;

- Lack of skills at the centre to interpret the information available;

- Rent-seeking and corrupt behaviour of central officials charged with enforcing central controls;

- Manipulation of data provided to the centre by local governments;

- Central regulations that create perverse incentives on the part of local officials (e.g. actions that avoid the intended effect of the regulations).

References and further reading

Blair, Harry (2000). 'Participation and Accountability at the Periphery: Democratic Local Governance in Six Countries', *World Development*, 28(1).

Crook, R. and Manor, J. (1998). *Democracy and Decentralisation in South Asia and West Africa: Participation, Accountability and Performance*. Cambridge: Cambridge University Press.

Crook, R and Sverrisson, A (2001). 'Decentralization and Poverty Alleviation in Developing Countries: A Comparative Analysis, or is West Bengal Unique?', IDS Working Paper 130. Brighton: Institute of Development Studies at the University of Sussex, http://www.ids.ac.uk/ids/bookshop/wp/wp130.pdf

Fjeldstad, O.-H. (2004). *Decentralisation and Corruption: A Review of the Literature*. Bergen, Norway: Chr. Michelson Institute.

Fukuyama, F. (2004). *State-Building: Governance and World Order in the 21st Century*. Ithaca, NY: Cornell University Press.

Heller, P. (2001). 'Moving the State: The Politics of Democratic Decentralization in Kerala, South Africa, and Porto Alegre', *Politics and Society* 29(1): 131–63.

Jütting, J. *et al.* (2004). 'Decentralisation and Poverty Reduction in Developing Countries: Exploring the Impact', Working Paper 236. Paris: OECD Development Centre, August, http://www.oecd.org/dataoecd/40/19/33648213.pdf

Manor, J. (1999). *The Political Economy of Democratic Decentralization*. Washington, DC: World Bank.

Mawhood, P. (ed.) (1993). *Local Government in the Third World: Experience of Decentralization in Tropical Africa*. Pretoria: Africa Institute of South Africa.

Oates, W. (1972). *Fiscal Federalism*. New York: Harcourt Brace Jovanovich.

OECD-DAC (2004). *Lessons Learnt on Donor Support to Decentralisation and Local Governance*, DAC Evaluation Series. Paris: OECD, http://www.oecd.org/dataoecd/46/60/30395116.pdf

Olowu, D. and Wunsch, J.S. (2004). *Local Governance in Africa: The Challenge of Democratic Decentralization*. Boulder, CO: Lynne Rienner.

Prud'homme, Rémy (1995). 'The Dangers of Decentralization', *World Bank Research Observer*, 10(2).

Rodríguez-Pose, A. and Gill, N. (2004). 'Is There a Global Link between Regional Disparities and Devolution?', *Environment and Planning A*, 36: 2097–2117.

Schneider, A. (2003). 'Who Gets What from Whom? The Impact of Decentralization on Tax Capacity and Pro-Poor Policy', IDS Working Paper 179, Brighton: Institute of Development Studies at the University of Sussex, http://www.gtzsfdm.or.id/documents/library/on_dec/Decentralisation_Poverty_ISDWorkingPaper_Feb2003.pdf

Tanzi, V. (2000). 'Fiscal Federalism and Decentralization: A Review of Some Efficiency and Macroeconomic Aspects', in Tanzi, V. (ed.), *Policies, Institutions and the Dark Side of Economics*. Cheltenham: Edward Elgar.

Tiebout, C.M. (1956). 'A Pure Theory of Local Expenditure', *Journal of Political Economy*, 64(5): 416–24.

Von Braun, J. and Grote, U. (2000). 'Does Decentralization Serve the Poor?' Paper for IMF Conference on Fiscal Decentralization. Washington, DC: International Monetary Fund, http://www.imf.org/external/pubs/ft/seminar/2000/fiscal/vonbraun.pdf

World Bank (1997). 'The State in a Changing World', in *World Development Report 1997*. Washington, DC: World Bank.

CHAPTER TWO

Revenue Sources for Local Government

Nick Devas

Why local governments need resources

Local governments need resources in order to finance the services and activities for which they are responsible. This may include the direct provision of goods and services where the market fails to provide satisfactorily (e.g. 'public goods' and 'merit goods', such as health and education), or contracting or subsidising the private sector to provide them. Local governments also have a variety of regulatory roles, such as building and development control and consumer protection, which have to be financed. Moreover, local governments may need to subsidise certain services for low-income groups, even though redistribution is generally regarded as primarily a function of central government.

Locally generated resources are also essential for another reason. One of the principal justifications for decentralisation is that the decisions made about local services will reflect the needs, priorities and willingness to pay of local citizens. Decisions about how much to tax local citizens, and how to use those tax revenues to provide services, are core elements of local democracy and critical to local accountability. This requires that local governments have under their control a range of local taxes and charges, borne by residents of the jurisdiction, to fund at least part of the cost of services which benefit those residents. It also requires that local decision-makers have a degree of discretion about the level of taxation.

However, the reality in most countries is that local revenue sources meet only part – sometimes quite a small part – of local expenditure needs. There are two reasons for this. Firstly, the most significant taxes (such as income tax, corporate profits tax, VAT, customs duties, excises) are usually assigned to central government. This is because central government is much better placed to collect such taxes uniformly, efficiently and equitably, particularly where tax revenues are collected in only certain locations (e.g. ports, in the case of customs duties). As a result, the taxes left for local government are generally small and often problematic (as will be discussed below). Secondly, the tax base is unevenly distributed within countries. While large cities may be able to generate substantial tax revenues, smaller, more remote and rural jurisdictions may have little scope for levying taxes. Therefore, local revenue raising needs to be accompanied by a system of fiscal transfers from the centre to ensure that local governments have sufficient resources to carry out their mandated functions, and to ensure that financial resources are equitably distributed between local governments.

In the Commonwealth, the dependence of local governments on intergovernmental transfers varies widely, ranging from 10 per cent in South Africa, 15 per cent in Malaysia, 20 per cent in Australia, 40 per cent in Canada, 70 per cent in Ghana, 78 per cent in Uganda and up to to 90 per cent in Lesotho, 98 per cent in Trinidad and Tobago and 100 per cent in Seychelles (CLGF, 2005). However, these averages disguise big differences within countries, typically between urban and rural local governments.

Thus, local revenue sources remain important as a way of financing part of local expenditure and to establish a degree of accountability to citizens for the expenditure decisions made by the local government. In most countries, much could be done to improve local revenues, through more efficient administration and assigning new revenue sources, as well as improving expenditure management so that the limited resources go further.

Revenue sources for local governments

The following are the main revenue sources for local governments.

a) **Local taxes** are in principle the main source of revenue for local governments, with the choice about tax rates to fund local services being the key annual decision made by local elected representatives. There are many types of local tax (see below), of which property tax is the most common internationally.

b) **Charges** for services provided, where a service is provided directly and exclusively to the payer; charges are normally related to the cost of providing the service.

c) **Fees for permits and licences**, where the prime purpose is to regulate an activity, rather than to raise revenue; the costs are normally (but not always) limited to the cost of administration/enforcement.

d) **Profits from local enterprises** – where the local government owns an enterprise, any profits from that enterprise would accrue to the local government (but so would any losses). This is still a significant revenue source for local governments in China but not in many other countries, although local governments in many countries, such as Pakistan and Uganda, own markets which are operated as commercial enterprises, and some countries also have municipal water enterprises.

e) **Central government revenue sharing** – shares of taxes (and other revenues) collected by central government and allocated (partly or wholly) to local government, either based on their origin (where they were collected) or by formula (see chapter 6).

f) **Intergovernmental grants** of various types to finance some of the costs of local government services, as well as equalising (to some extent) resources between local governments (see chapter 6).

g) **Borrowing** to finance capital expenditure, from various sources – banks, government, donors, bonds, etc. (see chapter 4). However, strictly speaking, borrowing is not a revenue source but a financing mechanism, since the money has to be repaid.

The principal sources of revenue in various local governments are shown in Box 2.1.

Box 2.1. Principal revenue sources for local government

1. Property tax (rates) on land and/or buildings
2. Tax on the transfer of immovable property
3. Tax on motor vehicles
4. Local sales tax and/or tax on the sale of local products
5. Tax on local businesses and services
6. Tax on electricity consumption
7. Tax on non-motorised vehicles
8. Tax on tourism, hotels, restaurants and entertainments
9. Tolls on roads, bridges, etc. within the limits of the local government
10. Charges for public works and public utilities like waste collection, drainage, sewerage and water supply
11. Charges for markets and rents for market stalls
12. Charges for the use of bus stations and taxi parks
13. Fees for approval of building plans, and erection and re-erection of buildings
14. Fees for fairs, agricultural shows, cattle fairs, industrial exhibitions, tournaments and other public events
15. Fees for licensing of businesses, professions and vocations
16. Fees for other licences or permits, and penalties or fines for violations
17. Fees for advertisements
18. Fees on sale of animals in cattle markets
19. Fees for registration and certification of births, marriages and deaths
20. Fees in respect of education and health facilities established or maintained by the local government
21. Fees for other specific services rendered by the local government
22. Rent for land, buildings, equipment, machinery and vehicles
23. Surpluses from local commercial enterprises
24. Interest on bank deposits or other funds

Closing the 'fiscal gap'

Local governments in most countries are seriously short of money to meet their expenditure needs. In order to bridge the 'fiscal gap', they need to examine a number of options:

a) *Reducing expenditure*

- Abandoning activities that are no longer necessary
- Privatising or contracting out some activities
- Operating more efficiently
- Improving budgeting and financial management.

b) *Improving revenue collection* (see chapter 3)

- Improving the identification of taxpayers and assessment of tax liabilities
- More effective collection and enforcement mechanisms
- Improving record keeping, accounting and checking arrangements
- More effective pursuit of arrears
- Reducing collection and compliance costs.

c) *Increasing charges for services*

- Charging for some services that are now free
- Reviewing charges in relation to service costs.

d) *Increased local tax revenues*

- Increasing tax rates
- Moving rates fixed in monetary amounts to *ad valorem* rates (i.e. rates based on the value of the taxed object)
- Identifying new local taxes (subject to central government approval).

e) *Negotiating for increased intergovernmental transfers*

f) *Borrowing*

- For investments that generate revenues, directly or indirectly
- Subject to local government borrowing capacity.

See Blore *et al.* (2004) for examples of improved financial performance by municipal governments.

Selecting local revenue sources

The choice of revenue sources for local government generally lies with central government (although it may be specified in the constitution). Decentralisation of functions should be accompanied by decentralisation of revenue sources. However, due account must be taken of the suitability of revenue sources for levy and collection at the local level. There are a number of criteria for selecting local tax instruments: the first five sets of criteria are general tax criteria, the sixth relates specifically to local taxes.

a) *Yield*

- The tax should be capable of generating a substantial revenue; in many developing countries, local governments have multiple small revenues that are little more than nuisance taxes.

- The yield should be stable and predictable year on year (the yield of some local taxes, e.g. on agricultural products, may be quite unstable, depending on local harvest conditions and world market prices).

- The yield should be elastic – that is, increasing automatically with inflation, increases in real incomes and population growth; *ad valorem* taxes are preferable to fixed monetary amounts; many local taxes, e.g. property taxes, are relatively inelastic, so that the real value of the revenue can fall over time.

b) *Collection costs*

- The proportion of the tax yield that is used up in collection costs should be low; some local taxes cost more to collect than they yield, which is obviously pointless and economically damaging. This situation may arise because the cost of collection is seldom examined against the revenue collected.

c) *Equity*

- The tax basis and liability should be clear, not arbitrary, thereby minimising risks of exploitation by tax collectors.

- Those in similar economic situations should be treated equally ('horizontal equity'); that is, someone earning $100 in agriculture should face the same tax bill as someone earning $100 in a shop. All too often, local taxes impinge only on particular sectors.

- The rich should pay more than the poor ('vertical equity' or 'ability to pay'); again, many local taxes impinge mainly on the (relatively) poor.

- Where a revenue is related to a particular service, those who benefit most should pay most ('the benefit principle of equity'); this provides the justification for benefit taxes (such as vehicle licences) and charging for services which not everyone receives.

There may often be a conflict between vertical equity and the benefit principle, since those who benefit from a service may well be those least able to pay.

d) *Economic efficiency/neutrality*

- Taxes should be neutral in their impact, not distorting relative prices more than necessary (unless the aim is to regulate consumption – e.g. taxes on cigarettes). Price distortions occur where certain commodities or activities are taxed and not others; some local taxes are levied on only certain commodities, e.g. certain agricultural products or goods entering a market or a jurisdiction, causing producers and consumers to alter their behaviour in an economically damaging way.

- Similarly, taxes should be designed to avoid creating unintended incentives or disincentives (again, unless the incentive/disincentive effect is intended). Taxes on incomes and profits create disincentives to work, savings and investment, while local toll barriers on roads may cause diversion of traffic to less suitable routes.

e) *Ability to implement*

- Taxes require political will to implement; this will be easier if the tax is not too 'visible' to the taxpayer. A local tax on electricity can be 'disguised' in the bill for electricity and so is less visible than a property tax demand; on the other hand, visibility is important for accountability, so that people know what they are paying in local taxes for what services.

- Taxes should be simple enough to be administered within the administrative capacity of local government; some taxes are easier to administer than others, and local governments generally have limited capacity to implement complex taxes.

f) *Is the tax suitable for local government?*

- Is it clear which local government should receive the tax? In the case of a property tax, it is clear in which jurisdiction the property is located, but with an income tax, should the tax be paid to the local government where taxpayers work or where they live? Since income taxes are generally collected through employers, assigning the revenue to the jurisdiction where the employee lives requires an elaborate administrative arrangement.

- Is the tax collected within the local jurisdiction? For example, a sales tax may be collected from the headquarters of the retail company, and thereby benefit a local government far from where the purchase was made or where the purchaser lives.

- Will the tax be paid solely or mainly by residents within the jurisdiction, rather than being 'exported' to those living elsewhere? A profits or turnover tax on a business which sells goods throughout the country could effectively be 'exported' to residents of many other local governments, thereby breaking the link between those who benefit from the tax-funded expenditure and those who bear the burden of the tax.

- Can all local authorities benefit from the tax or will the tax exaggerate economic differences between regions? For example, customs duties would benefit only those places where ports and airports are located, while a local tourism tax only benefits tourist areas.

- Is some local discretion over tax rates possible without causing locational distortions? For example, it would be difficult to have differential local taxes on petrol, since some motorists would simply drive to the lower tax jurisdiction.

From this last set of considerations, it is apparent that the main taxes, notably VAT or sales tax, profits tax and customs duties cannot realistically be levied at the local level, and that the most suitable *local* taxes are those where the tax base is wholly confined within a jurisdiction, is immobile and is relatively similar in all jurisdictions. This is why property tax is the most common form of local taxation.

There are, of course, inherent conflicts between some of these criteria. For example, making a tax more vertically equitable may also make it less neutral (e.g. higher taxes on luxuries), as well as making it more complex to administer. No tax is perfect: the aim should be to select those that perform best overall, or do least damage.

Ideally, local governments should have a combination of local taxes – some which score well on certain criteria and others which score well on others; however, they should not have too many taxes – say three to four – to avoid perceptions of 'nuisance taxation'.

Principal forms of local taxation

As already noted, property taxation (in various forms) is the most common form of local taxation around the world. This will be discussed in more detail below.

There are many other local taxes used in different countries with varying degrees of success.

Local income tax: Potentially the most equitable form of taxation and used in several European countries. But progressive income taxes are generally administered more equitably and efficiently at national level, especially where the formal sector is small and largely concentrated in the capital city, as is the case in many developing countries. However, a few African countries (notably Uganda) have developed forms of *mass personal taxation* for local government. These apply a graduated tax scale on incomes below the national income tax threshold. Incomes, especially from agriculture and the informal sector, are assessed on a presumptive basis (i.e. the likely income from a particular activity or piece of land) rather than on actual incomes, which may be hard to determine. This can be expensive to administer, given the numbers involved. It can also involve inequities if not well co-ordinated with the national income tax system, especially since there is usually a flat-rate minimum for all (so making it effectively a poll tax for the poorest).

Poll tax: Flat rate taxes on every adult (or every working adult) were common in colonial times in Africa. While relatively easy to administer, they are clearly regressive and are consequently unpopular and difficult to enforce. As a result, they have largely been abandoned. An experiment with poll tax (called the community charge) in Britain in the 1990s was abandoned because of perceived unfairness, high evasion rates and high collection costs, but above all because of its unpopularity.

Taxes on agricultural land are widely used in Asia to fund local government in rural areas, but are of declining importance. They require an elaborate system of valuation of land, and the yield may be relatively small if the land and/or the people are poor. They also tend to be strongly resisted by landowners (who may often have powerful influence over policy).

Taxes on local products, notably agricultural produce, are easy and cheap to administer where there is a state monopoly produce marketing organisation, but where such arrangements have been abandoned (as is now usually the case) they can be difficult to administer and are wide open to corruption. Such taxes can create serious disincentives to production and marketing of produce, and incentives to smuggling between local government areas if tax rates differ. They also create problems of horizontal equity (e.g. between producers of taxed and untaxed products) and of inter-regional equity (e.g. between regions with a high output of taxable products and other regions).

Taxes (royalties) on extraction of minerals and materials: While minerals and other natural resources are usually taxed by central government (not always in a transparent manner), there may be scope for local governments to benefit. This could be through local taxes or charges, or shares of national taxes (as in the case of oil revenues in Indonesia). It is common for local governments to levy charges for the extraction of sand, gravel, timber and other building materials from the local area. In Sierra Leone, chiefdoms have rights to revenues from diamond mining and local governments are supposed to get a share of this. The obvious problem is how to monitor extraction and assess the value of the materials extracted from (usually) remote locations; the greater the value of the materials, the greater the risks of collusion and smuggling.

Local sales tax can be used for large jurisdictions (e.g. states in the USA and India), but differences in local sales tax rates can have undesirable effects on the pattern of economic activity (e.g. cross-boundary transactions). In most countries sales taxes are best administered nationally. Where VAT is adopted, local administration is not really possible because of the integrated nature of the tax (i.e. problems of differential rates between jurisdictions and how to share revenue between jurisdictions – problems that are apparent with state-levied VAT in Brazil).

Octroi: A tax on the movement of goods into a jurisdiction (effectively, a local customs duty) which has been an important source of municipal revenue in some states of India (and of Pakistan in the past). However, it has hugely damaging effects on internal trade and economic efficiency, and cannot be recommended.

Local taxes on businesses: Many countries (e.g. Germany, France, Hungary, Brazil, Philippines and South Africa) have some form of tax on local businesses, particularly on services. These may be levied on turnover or profits – either presumed or actual. Such taxes can generate substantial revenues, but there are problems in making correct assessments. There are also possible overlaps with national taxes or a local property tax, as well as issues of tax exporting and disincentives to local economic development.

Businesses licences are the commonest form of local business taxation, particularly in Africa. They were originally a form of regulation, but in practice are now a significant source of local revenue in many countries. They are relatively easy to assess and collect, if kept simple, but they can have a negative effect on the local economy if they are set too high and the equity effects are uncertain (depending on who bears the ultimate burden of the tax). In order to generate more revenue without impinging unduly on small businesses or the poor, there is a need to relate in some way the amounts paid to turnover or profitability: this creates assessment problems, with risks of corruption and collusion. The single business permit system in Kenya has been successful in increasing revenue from this source through a progressive tariff scale based on relatively crude but easily verified indicators (Kelly and Devas, 2001). (See Box 2.2.)

Taxes on tourism and entertainments, e.g. hotels, restaurants, cinemas and sports events. These taxes are common in Europe and several other parts of the world, and can produce a reasonable yield in the main urban centres and tourist areas. They are relatively easy to administer and crudely equitable, since they fall mainly on the rich, as well as visitors who use local services, but are somewhat non-neutral since they fall on certain sectors only.

Taxes on utilities, notably electricity, are a local tax that is increasingly used because of the ease and cheapness of administration. It is levied as a surcharge on the utility bill and collected by the utility company on behalf of the local government. It is relatively equitable, since the rich consume far more electricity than the poor. However, it can have an adverse effect on economic efficiency by distorting utility prices, and can only be applied in regions that have electricity.

Taxes on motor vehicles: Annual vehicle taxes (and transfer taxes) can generate a substantial yield, especially in larger cities. They are relatively easy to administer and can be regarded as equitable and politically acceptable. However, central governments are often reluctant to surrender this revenue source, even though local governments may be responsible for the maintenance of local roads and streets.

They are more appropriate to large jurisdictions (e.g. provinces, as in Indonesia), since vehicles tend to be registered in the urban centres, but use roads beyond the urban jurisdiction.

Tax on vehicle fuel (usually levied as a surcharge on a national fuel tax) is very easy and cheap to collect (centrally, through the oil companies). The tax is borne mainly by the rich, and it may have a marginal effect on reducing fuel use. However, it is likely to benefit mainly the developed regions and urban centres, where fuel stations are located. Revenue sharing by formula of a centrally administered tax (such as the fuel levy introduced in a number of African countries) is more appropriate than a directly collected local tax.

Betterment taxes or valorisation charges: These taxes seek to capture from land owners or developers some of the increase in land values that results from urban development and the provision of infrastructure. They are widely used in Latin America to finance urban infrastructure. Depending on how they are implemented, they are usually equitable, but they may be complex to administer, may create unintended inequities and are likely to be politically sensitive.

Market charges, bus/taxi park charges and car parking charges: Technically these are charges (or fees), not taxes, but in practice the charge is often raised well above the costs of the service, making it effectively a tax on the particular activity. In many African countries, market charges are the principal revenue sources for small and rural local governments as they are relatively easy to collect (and collection is often contracted out). The impact of market and bus/taxi park charges is generally regressive, and high charges create incentives for activities to be shifted away from the designated location. By contrast, car parking charges can be regarded as relatively equitable and ensure more efficient use of available space, but they are only feasible in major urban centres.

Other local taxes: Around the world one can find numerous other local taxes – on radios, bicycles, dogs, outdoor advertising, alcohol and particular local products, as well as road tolls. Few of these raise any significant amount of revenue and they may cost more to collect than they yield; they are often regressive and may be economically damaging.

Property taxation

Property taxation is the most common form of local taxation worldwide. In many countries it contributes more than half of local government revenue.

Strengths of property tax: The property tax has several merits as a local tax:

• It has a substantial, stable and predictable yield;

• It is crudely equitable, in that rich people generally occupy more valuable properties than the poor;

Box 2.2. Raising more local revenue from business taxation in Kenya

Business licences can be costly to business

Business licences are imposed at local level in many countries, both rich and poor. Licensing was originally seen as a regulatory instrument to protect customers, workers or competitors. The fee imposed for the licence is often small, but the red tape involved may impose high compliance costs on businesses, especially where they are required to have multiple licences for the different aspects of their business.

In Kenya, by the late 1990s, the business licensing system had become very unsatisfactory. The licence fee schedule was determined for each municipality through negotiation with central government, but the fees set for different businesses bore no relation to their ability to pay. In order to obtain a licence, businesses had to meet a number of pre-conditions, such as obtaining a health clearance certificate. This could be a time-consuming process, with ample opportunity for rent-seeking on the part of the officials concerned. Moreover, businesses were often required to have multiple licences, including in many cases licences from both the local and the central government. There was huge dissatisfaction with the system among businesses.

Licensing may generate declining revenues

In Kenya, business licences did not cover all businesses and the inefficiencies of the system meant that many were not included. Because of the limited variation in tariffs, the amount of revenue which could be generated was constrained by the ability to pay of the smallest informal sector business. Increases in tariffs rarely kept pace with inflation, so that revenue declined in real terms. By the 1990s the system had ossified. It neither regulated businesses well nor raised significant revenues for local government.

Simplifying the system

Instead of abolition, the system was changed into a purely revenue function under the title of single business permit (SBP). This required central government policy and legal change to:

• De-link the payment of the fee from regulatory 'clearances'

• Broaden the base to include all businesses

• Simplify the tariff structure and make it significantly more progressive by relating it to indicators of size or profitability

• Establish 'one stop shops' to issue the new permits

- Require the purchase of only one permit for each business premises

- Remove the business licensing function from central government.

Although the shape of the new SBP has been centrally designed, local authorities have discretion to select an appropriate set of tariffs from a range of pre-approved and internally consistent tariff sets. This has secured municipal engagement. The SBP was also launched as a business-friendly initiative as part of wider deregulation reform.

Capacity building to support the change

The SBP registration forms are simple and are based on self-assessment by the business. Municipalities have been helped to survey businesses and initiate a registration drive. This has helped to increase coverage. Training was provided to assist municipalities to work closely with local businesses and to select the appropriate tariff set. This, together with the removal of the requirement for multiple licences and the de-linking of SBP from subjective regulatory clearances, has improved compliance.

Initial results and lessons

By 2000 all municipalities had introduced the SBP. Within two years revenues had increased by over 30 per cent and in some municipalities had doubled, although collection is still a problem in many places. Revenue improvements have stemmed partly from increased coverage and partly from enhanced tariffs, although some local authorities were forced by their local business community to reduce the high tariffs that they had adopted in the first round. But collection efforts are now based on a more acceptable form of business taxation, revenues have increased and businesses are benefiting from reduced compliance costs.

Reproduced from Blore, Devas and Slater, 2004

- It has no serious effects on relative prices or incentives, and hence on economic efficiency (although there may be a certain disincentive to development, but there is also a positive incentive to more efficient use of land and buildings);

- The basis is reasonably clear and understandable to taxpayers;

- Property is immovable, so the tax object cannot be hidden;

- It is relatively easy to administer;

- There are no problems in assigning the revenue to the correct local government;

- Local governments can have discretion over tax rates;

- It can benefit all local governments, since land and property exist everywhere, although it tends to benefit urban areas more than rural areas.

Weaknesses: Property taxation has certain disadvantages:

- The yield is relatively inelastic – in particular, yields only increase in line with inflation if properties are revalued or if the tariff is increased, and doing this involves difficult political decisions;

- The relationship between the tax bill and ability to pay is crude: there may be serious inequities, e.g. where poor people live in relatively expensive property;

- The payment is highly visible and cannot be disguised, so that there is a reluctance to pay and a reluctance by decision-makers to increase the tariff;

- There has to be a system of property valuation which requires skills, and revaluation has to take place regularly. In rural areas, property may not be titled or recorded on a cadastre, and so is not captured in a valuation roll, while in urban areas informal settlements are often not included;

- The potentially large number of taxpayers means that there is a substantial administrative task;

- Enforcement can be difficult, especially against big property owners and politicians;

- High tax rates can be a disincentive to development, and can encourage people and businesses to move to lower tax jurisdictions.

Property tax assessment: The calculation of the property tax bill has three elements:

- Valuation of the property;

- Tax rate or tariff, expressed as a percentage of the valuation;

- Assessment for a particular property, which is the product of the valuation multiplied by the tax rate.

Exemptions: There may be various categories of exemption – low-value properties (see below); government properties (but it is normal for governments to make a payment in lieu of tax, since local governments still have to provide services to government buildings); places of worship; charities; and social facilities. There is a risk that the range of exemptions will become large, while exempt buildings still require the local government to provide services.

Property tax registers need to be updated regularly. It is common to find that large amounts of property have never been included in the register. Aerial surveys and GIS (geographic information systems) can be used to produce and update property cadastres, but these need to be supplemented by on-the-ground inspection.

Valuation may be done by the local government or by central government. The tariff rate may be set at the discretion of the local government, or central government may specify the tariff (or more commonly specify a range or a ceiling). Worldwide, the tariffs for property tax vary considerably, but typically tariffs are in the range 0.2–2 per cent of capital value.

Valuations may be based on:

• Annual value method (the annual rental income which is obtained from renting that property, or which could be obtained from renting it if it were rented);

• Capital value method (the actual – or potential – sale price of the property on the market).

The method chosen will partly depend on what data are available. In either case, not every property may be valued individually: if there are many similar properties, valuations may be made on a sample basis. Valuations should take account of differences between properties in terms of location, size of land, quality of land, permitted land use, size of building, type of construction, etc.

Valuation rolls should be published in order to discourage collusion between assessors and taxpayers.

Mass appraisal: Where valuation skills are limited, mass appraisal should be used. This system categorises properties roughly by type, location and size, and assigns approximate relative values to each category, either per property or per square metre of property. Once the basic classification is done, valuations of groups of property can be done quickly and cheaply by unskilled staff using a table of values. Valuations do not need to be accurate in an absolute sense, only fair relative to each other. (The UK's council tax banding system is a form of mass appraisal.)

Site value or improved site tax? Assessments may be based on site value only, or on improved site value (i.e. land plus buildings). The former (used in Commonwealth countries such as Kenya, South Africa and Jamaica) has the advantages of stimulating development, encouraging efficient use of land and discouraging speculative land holding. The disadvantages are that site value rating may be seen as being less fair (since the owner of a high-rise building would pay the same as the owner of a single storey building on a similar-sized and adjacent plot), and may raise less revenue. It may encourage overdevelopment of land and may be more complex to administer (since it requires the maximum permitted use to be determined for every plot). A compromise approach is to tax both land and buildings, but to levy a higher rate of tax on land than on buildings.

Owner or occupier? The property tax may be levied on the owner or the occupier. In the case of tenanted property, the tax burden will ultimately be shared between owner and occupier through adjustments to the rent payable; the relative shares will depend on the elasticity of the supply of and demand for rented property. The advantage of levying the tax on the occupier is that the occupier is resident, whereas the owner may be difficult to trace. The disadvantage of levying the tax on the occupier is that they may leave, obliging the local government to pursue them, whereas a liability on the owner can become a charge on the property, such that the property cannot be sold without the tax being paid. The ideal arrangement may be to levy the tax initially on the occupier, with a residual liability on the owner if the occupier fails to pay.

Exemption of low value properties: In some countries (e.g. Indonesia), low-value properties are exempt. This reduces the administrative burden of assessment and collection of small amounts of tax. It may also help to protect the poor, although where such properties are rented, the main beneficiary may be the landlord, who can charge a higher rent in the absence of the tax.

Other assessments: Property tax assessments may also provide the basis for special assessments, for example charges for water (as historically in the UK) or for waste collection. They may also be used as a basis for charging property owners for contributions towards infrastructure improvements, such as new or improved roads in their vicinity.

Local choices over local taxation

As already noted, one of the principles of decentralised governance is a degree of local choice over the amount of tax raised from local citizens to finance local services. This does not mean that all local expenditures have to be financed from local revenues (i.e. financial self-sufficiency of local governments). Rather, what matters is 'discretion at the margin': that is, that local governments should have sufficient choice over a sufficient amount of local taxes to be able to make decisions about marginal differences in local expenditure. Since the bulk of expenditure is largely pre-determined (by statutory requirements, central regulation, historical conditions, etc.), in practice local governments only have a real choice over quite a small proportion of their expenditure budget – perhaps 10–20 per cent. Therefore, discretion over local taxation needs to reflect at least that range of expenditure choice.

It is normal for central governments to determine the range of taxes to be assigned to local government, and the definition of the bases for those taxes. In some systems, local governments have some discretion about introducing new local taxes, but that is highly problematic, since new taxes may overlap with existing national or local taxes, may be non-neutral and inequitable in their impact, and may undermine national fiscal stability.

Local governments may have discretion over assessments and exemptions. Again, there is a case for central assessment of some taxes, in order that the basis for taxation is uniform across the country. Differences in assessments and exemptions between jurisdictions can lead to an undesirable shifting of tax objects between jurisdictions. On the other hand, exemptions can be used by local governments to stimulate local economic development, although they may also be used to give favourable treatment corruptly.

The important area for local discretion is over the tax rate. This should be the main political choice that the local government makes each year, to set the rate so as to generate sufficient revenue to meet its expenditures. Central governments often seek to limit this choice, e.g. by setting ceilings on tax rates. Apart form the negative effect on local autonomy, which may already be quite limited, such limits can seriously constrain local revenues where the ceilings on tax rates are not adjusted for inflation. For example, in the case of property tax, local governments may soon reach the ceiling rate, after which no increase in revenue is possible.

In addition to local collection of the revenue (where the effectiveness and efficiency of the revenue collection service will determine the resources available to the local government), the other main area of local discretion is in the use of the tax revenues. In principle, local governments have full discretion in the use of local revenues, in accordance with statutory obligations, although even here the central government may seek to direct or influence local government spending patterns.

Apart from local own revenues, local governments may benefit from the national tax base in other ways. One is surcharging national taxes (also called tax-base sharing). This is where the local government is empowered to add a percentage to a national tax, such as income tax. This model is common in Scandinavia. Although the tax base is set by central government and the revenue is collected by the centre, the local government has a choice (within limits) over the tax rate and over the use of the money. This then approximates to a local tax.

The other method is the sharing of nationally collected taxes. Where revenues are shared by origin, the revenue reflects the local tax base and the local government has a strong incentive to assist in revenue mobilisation. Where the revenue sharing is by formula, that incentive is greatly reduced and the outcome is much more like a grant than a local tax.

Charges and fees for services

Charges are normally made for local government services that are provided directly and exclusively to the beneficiary (i.e. 'private' goods), for example piped water and recreation facilities. By contrast, 'public goods' (e.g. police and street lighting, which are non-rival and non-excludable) should normally be financed by taxation. The problem is that many services that local governments provide have both 'public' and 'private' characteristics, e.g. education, health services, waste collection and public toilets, and require at least a degree of subsidy.

Justifications for charging for services: These include:

- The need to ration demand for a service and avoid waste;

- The need to provide the resources to maintain and increase the supply of the service;

- The 'benefit principle' of equity – where the benefits are private, those who benefit from a service should pay for the service, rather than those who do not benefit.

However, there are also arguments against charging:

- Administrative difficulties and costs in levying a charge, since non-payers have to be excluded and the amount consumed has to be measured. For example, water meters have to be installed, maintained and read, and illegal connections prevented;

- 'Externalities' – the fact that some services benefit the public at large, as well as the individual beneficiary (e.g. immunisation, waste collection);

- The poor cannot afford to pay for the necessary level of services (e.g. health, education).

A decision not to charge for a service is a decision to subsidise that service. Such a decision needs to be explicit, justified on the basis of externalities (public benefits) and/or poverty reduction (if it is certain that the poor – and only the poor – will benefit). All too often, services that are supposedly free (e.g. health services) do not exist in practice or are of a very low quality, because there are no resources to maintain or improve the service. Also, subsidised services intended for the poor may actually benefit mainly the better off (for example, piped water supplies benefit only those connected to the system, whereas the poor, who are not connected, receive no benefit), or are captured by those responsible for allocating the subsidised goods ('rent-seeking' by those who control access).

Pricing policy: It is normally advocated that charges for services should be set to recover the costs of the service, or – more correctly – to recover the marginal costs (that is, the additional cost of serving the particular consumer). However, there are problems in setting the price correctly, due to lack of disaggregated cost data and issues about short-run or long-run marginal costs. Again, there will be cases where subsidy is appropriate, where public benefits are significant or where the service is provided exclusively, or mainly, for the poor. This may require a form of product differentiation, to ensure that what is provided for the poor is not used by the better off; for example, public standpipes for water are likely to be of interest only to low-income groups.

Cross-subsidies: It may be possible to address the needs of the poor through internal cross-subsidies, at least up to a point. However, that depends on being able to differentiate customers according to income (at least approximately), and ensuring that the rich do not access the services designed for the poor. There will always be limits to the extent of cross-subsidy, since if the price to the rich is raised too high, they may seek alternative supplies (e.g. a private borehole for water) and opt out of the cross-subsidised public system.

Fees: In the case of fees for permits and licences, where the primary purpose is regulation, the costs involved may be small (administrative and inspection costs). It may be considered appropriate to set a fee higher than these costs on the grounds that: (a) the licence or permit is a rationing device; and (b) that the permit/licence holder may derive financial benefits from having the permit/licence. In some cases, fees can be used as a form of taxation, by setting the tariff well above costs (e.g. car parking), in which case consideration must be given to the equity effects on those who pay, as well as any disincentive effects. Where the primary purpose of the permit/licence is to control an activity, fee levels should not be set so high as to discourage people from applying, thereby defeating the main purpose of the permit/licence.

References

Blore, I., Devas, N. and Slater, R. (2004). *Municipalities and Finance: A Sourcebook for Capacity Building*. London: Earthscan.

Commonwealth Local Government Forum (2005). *Commonwealth Local Government Handbook*. London: CLGF.

Kelly, R. and Devas, N. (2001). 'Regulation or Revenues: An Analysis of Local Business Licences, with a Case Study of the Single Business Permit in Kenya', *Public Administration and Development*, 21: 381–91.

CHAPTER THREE
Local Revenue Administration

Nick Devas

Introduction

Tax reform requires improvements in tax administration as much as reform of tax policy (Bird and de Jantscher, 1992). The design of suitable local revenue sources (local taxes, charges, fees, etc.) must be matched by the ability of local government to administer and collect the revenue. In practice, in many developing and transition countries, performance in revenue collection is extremely poor. For the purposes of this chapter, we will refer primarily to local taxes, but the issues are similar for other revenue sources, and for all sub-national levels of government.

Local revenue administration has a number of stages:

- Tariff setting

- Taxpayer identification

- Assessment of an individual taxpayer's liability

- Collection of the tax due

- Enforcement against defaulters

- Accounting for the tax collected

- Reporting on and monitoring the results.

Local governments need to be concerned with the performance of their revenue administration. There are three possible indicators of performance.

Tax effort: The amount of tax collected compared with the economic base or taxable capacity of the local economy – taxable capacity being a measure of the size of the local economy which is amenable to local taxation. Gross regional domestic product (GRDP) is often used as a measure of taxable capacity, so that tax effort would compare actual local tax revenue against GRDP. However, the ability of the sub-national or local government to tax the local economy will depend on the tax instruments available to it – something that is generally outside its control. For example, the GRDP of the jurisdiction might be high because it is an oil-producing region, but the local government may have no instruments to tax the oil sector. Tax effort is the outcome of both tax policy (types of taxes, tax rates, etc.) and tax administration (effectiveness of tax administration). Local tax policy has been discussed in chapter 2, and is largely outside the control of local government (e.g. in the choice of taxes and setting tax bases).

Effectiveness:[1] the proportion of the tax potential that is realised. Tax potential is defined as the total amount which should be collected from each local tax levied at its specified rate if everyone pays the full amount for which they are liable:

$$\text{effectiveness} = \frac{\text{actual yield}}{\text{tax potential}} \times 100\%$$

Efficiency: the proportion of the tax collected which is used up in the cost of collection and administration:

$$\text{efficiency} = \frac{\text{collection cost}}{\text{actual yield}} \times 100\%$$

Effectiveness

One hundred per cent effectiveness would mean that all the tax potential was collected on time and accounted for in the local government budget. The problem is how to define potential. In most cases, we do not know the potential of a tax, because:

• Not all taxpayers have been identified;

• Not all taxpayers have been correctly assessed;

• There is discretion over tariffs, which means that there is no 'absolute' figure for potential.

Potential: For certain taxes we may have a reasonable indication of potential; for example, where the central government carries out assessments for property tax, local governments can regard the valuation roll as the measure of tax potential.

In the absence of such 'objective' measures, it may be possible to derive some indicator of potential from published statistics, e.g. sectoral GRDP statistics may give an indication of the tax potential for a tax on that sector; household expenditure statistics for an income tax; statistics on car sales/registrations for motor vehicle taxes; population statistics for a poll tax, etc. Although such statistics may not give a precise measure of potential, they can at least indicate if things are seriously wrong.

The main factors which threaten effectiveness:

• Failure to increase tax rates in line with inflation (unless tax rates are *ad valorem*);

• Failure to keep tax registers up-to-date with population and economic growth;

• Evasion by the taxpayer;

• Collusion between taxpayer and tax official;

Financing Local Government

- Delays in payment;

- Fraud by the tax official.

These are discussed further in the next section, in terms of the stages in tax administration.

Stages in an effective revenue administration system

Tariff setting: Ideally, tax yields should increase automatically with inflation, e.g. through an *ad valorem* basis (i.e. tax as a percentage of the price); where taxes, charges or fees are fixed in money terms, there should be a regular mechanism to review tax and charge rates, for example a review procedure as part of the annual budget or indexation to the retail price index.

Taxpayer identification: It should be difficult for taxpayers to conceal their identity. This can be facilitated where:

- Payment is automatic, e.g. a surcharge on an electricity bill;

- There is an inducement for people to identify themselves, e.g. people entering a cinema have to have a ticket which includes the tax;

- Identification can be linked to some other source of information, e.g. vehicle or land transfer information can be used to identify vehicle and property taxpayers;

- Liability is very obvious, e.g. the number of market stalls.

Identification is more difficult where the liability is easily disguised or where there is no objective data on tax objects, e.g. informal sector incomes or possession of a radio.

Assessment of the correct tax liability must be done either by the taxpayer (self assessment) or the tax official, or jointly. This involves both identifying the correct value of the tax object and applying the correct tariff.

This is helped where:

- Assessment is automatic, e.g. pay-as-you-earn (PAYE) income tax or a fixed percentage addition to hotel bills;

- Tariffs are widely known and the assessor has little discretion, e.g. standard charges for market stalls;

- There are other records which can be used as a check, e.g. types and prices of vehicles sold as a check on vehicle taxes;

- The functions of assessment and collection are separated, and there is a system of checking on assessments;

- Penalties for under-declaration and for collusion are high and the risk of being caught is high enough to be a deterrent.

The more scope there is for discretion on the part of the assessor, and for contact between taxpayer and assessor, the greater the risk of under-assessment.

Collection: The full amount should be collected at the earliest opportunity. This can be assisted where:

- Payment is automatic, e.g. an entry charge to a facility or pre-payment meters;
- Payment can be induced, e.g. where tax clearance certificates are required before contracts or licences can be obtained;
- Incentives are offered for prompt payment (but these can be costly);
- Penalties for late payment are sufficiently high and sufficiently probable to be a deterrent.

Enforcement may involve:

- Fines for late payment
- Publication of the names of defaulters
- Prosecution through the courts
- Seizure of assets
- Attachment of earnings (where a person is employed, the requirement that the employer deducts the debts from the person's wages, i.e. at source deduction)
- In extreme cases, imprisonment.

Enforcement of penalties and sanctions needs to be carried through to the logical conclusion, including court action and seizure of property, at least in a few exemplary cases, in order for defaulters to know that the local government is serious.

Effective enforcement requires:

- Administrative systems that identify the need for enforcement action in a timely way and follow through the required stages;
- Political support for enforcement action, which may be difficult to obtain;
- Legal/court processes that are efficient and are not unduly costly.

Accounting procedures: Proper accounting procedures are required to ensure that all the money collected is paid into the local government's Treasury and appears in the government's accounts. This requires:

- Adequate security arrangements to prevent loss or theft of cash, e.g. receipting systems, locks on safes and cash boxes;

- Proper book-keeping records, with arrangements for cross-checking by different officers;

- A system of auditing;

- A system of reporting on performance against potential (or targets), with follow-up action.

Efficiency

This measures the proportion of the tax yield which is used up in administering the tax. The cost of administration includes not only the direct cost of assessing and collecting the tax, but also indirect and overhead costs to the local government as a whole, e.g. police, court and other costs of taking enforcement measures.

In many cases, administration costs are not properly considered, since they are included under a different budget head from the revenues, so that comparison may be difficult. As a result, collection costs may actually absorb a large part of the revenue collected. This means that the local tax system is just a burden on local citizens without producing benefits.

The calculation of efficiency discussed so far is about average collection costs. Ideally, average collection costs should not exceed 5–10 per cent of revenue, although given the limited revenue sources of local governments in many countries, somewhat higher collection costs may be acceptable. There is also the question of the marginal cost of collection, that is, how much extra it costs to collect this additional dollar of tax revenue. It clearly makes no sense to spend more that $1 to collect $1 of revenue. However, it may still be appropriate to spend quite a high proportion at the margin (i.e. on the last dollar collected), since enforcement costs for the last dollar collected my be quite high but the credibility of the whole system depends on effective enforcement action. There will always be a balance to be struck on how much it is worth spending to collect that last dollar of revenue.

Compliance costs: It should be noted that there are also compliance costs to the taxpayer (travel costs to the tax office, time taken filling in forms and waiting, etc.), and costs in terms of public good will. Compliance costs for local taxes can often be very high, as taxpayers have to queue up to pay multiple small taxes. In addition, there may be 'unofficial costs' demanded by officials issuing licences and permits, which may greatly increase the costs to the taxpayer. Yet these compliance costs are rarely considered. While these are not costs to the local government, they are part of the overall burden of the local tax system and can have a detrimental effect on the local economy, as well as on the willingness of taxpayers to pay.

Efficiency can be assisted where:

- Assessment and collection are automatic, e.g. a fixed percentage addition to a bill;

- Several levies can be assessed or collected simultaneously;

- Collection can be linked to some other administrative process, e.g. a surcharge on a utilities bill;

- The tax liability is large, since the concern is with the proportion of the tax used up in administration.

Where taxes have to be paid in cash, the use of accessible facilities such as banks and post offices will reduce the compliance costs to the taxpayer and make it more likely that the tax will be paid. Collecting taxes door-to-door may increase yield, but the costs are enormous.

Incentives to tax officials, and to taxpayers for prompt payment, may increase yield, but may significantly increase costs.

There is obviously a trade-off between increasing effectiveness and efficiency, since the marginal costs of each additional dollar of tax revenue may be quite high. It is always possible to increase yield (effectiveness) by increasing collection costs (and hence reducing efficiency).

Effective and efficient revenue administration practices

Taxpayer identification

Maximum use should be made of records held by other agencies and departments (including central government tax departments) that give information about tax objects or subjects, e.g. business licence applications, transfers of ownership, etc.

Where there are multiple local taxes, a unified tax roll which brings together a taxpayer's liabilities to various taxes can be helpful. Computerisation can assist in cross-checking a taxpayer's liability for different taxes.

There will be a need for periodic field surveys to ensure that all tax objects have been included; in situations of rapid population growth and economic expansion, it is not enough to rely on existing tax rolls or to assume that new tax objects or taxpayers will be added to the list automatically.

Assessment

As many taxes and charges as possible should have an automatic assessment system (e.g. a surcharge to a bill or a fixed entry charge). Where there is likely to be contact between assessor and payer, the amount of discretion available to the assessor should be minimised.

Where possible, the functions of assessment and collection should be separated and staff rotated between jobs on a regular basis, to avoid 'cosy relationships' building up between taxpayers and officials.

Tax and charge rates should be publicly displayed to avoid overcharging by officials. In some cases (e.g. property tax), publication of assessments and valuation rolls can help to avoid collusion between tax official and taxpayer, since people can then see how neighbours or competitors are being assessed.

There should be regular checking of assessments by senior staff, on a random basis, with severe penalties if collusion is revealed.

Pre-printing by the local revenue office of tickets and invoices which are used to collect local taxes (e.g. for hotels or cinemas) may help to avoid under-declaration, but such pre-printed tickets and invoices must be held securely.

Penalties for under-declaration of self-assessed taxes should be sufficiently severe and probable to be a real deterrent.

Collection

Where possible, local taxes and charges should be designed to ensure full payment at the earliest date. Pre-payment meters, e.g. for water and electricity charges, are one way of doing this.

Penalties for late or non-payment should be sufficiently high and sufficiently probable to be a deterrent. Enforcement measures (e.g. attachment of earnings, seizure of property or, where all else fails, imprisonment) should be carried to their logical conclusion sufficiently frequently to avoid the system falling into disrepute. Incentives to taxpayers for prompt payment may be worthwhile, but at a cost.

Money collected should be paid into the local government's Treasury or the bank on a regular (e.g. daily) basis.

Checking and accounting

The whole system should contain adequate checks and controls. In particular, the system of recording assessments and payments should be straightforward and amenable to checking. Independent checks should be carried out as a matter of routine on the money received as compared with the relevant tax assessments.

Senior management should carry out spot checks at regular intervals, and ensure that any discrepancies are followed up and action taken against the staff responsible. All receipts must have a proper numbering system and must be held securely to prevent improper issuing.

Reporting

There should be a proper system for reporting on revenue performance. This should include information on yield compared to potential/assessment/target for the period concerned. This information should be produced regularly (monthly or quarterly) and submitted, in a timely manner, to those in a position to take action if there appears to be a problem.

There should also be regular reporting on enforcement measures taken, the level of arrears, progress in dealing with arrears, collection costs, etc.

Targets

Targets are sometimes used by revenue offices both as a stimulus to revenue effort and a guide to performance. Their effectiveness will depend on how they are set. If they are merely based on previous performance, rather than on revenue potential, they may not produce the required increase in yield (and may even discourage it, if an increased yield is seen merely to result in a higher target the following year).

Thus, targets should be based on a proper estimate of revenue potential. If the potential is so far above the previous year's realisations as to be unattainable within one year, a series of staged targets aimed at bringing yields up towards potential over a period of years should be devised.

Raising the public's tax consciousness

There is an important educational role to be played in making the public aware of the need to pay their taxes promptly. This can best be done by providing proper information on how revenues are used and by eliminating obvious examples of waste.

Soliciting the help of community leaders in presenting the information and exhorting the community to pay its taxes may have some positive results, particularly if community leaders feel they have some input into the decision-making process about how resources are to be used, and if the resources are seen to be of direct benefit to the local community.

Making it easy for people to pay, e.g. enabling taxes to be paid through banks and post offices, and avoiding unnecessary forms and bureaucracy, can help. Eliminating overlapping taxes that yield little, but require repeated demands on the taxpayer, can also help.

The public should be encouraged to demand a receipt or ticket for any payment made, in order to discourage fraud by collectors; in some cases lotteries using such tickets can provide an incentive to the public to demand tickets or receipts.

Computerisation

The great progress made in recent years in computer technology, and the rapid fall in costs, mean that there is enormous scope for the use of computer technology in the administration of most taxes. Many tasks in this field readily lend themselves to computerisation:

- Preparation of tax rolls

- Preparation of bills

- Receipting of bills

- Checking accounts

- Checking receipts against assessments

- Preparing lists of defaulters

- Preparing regular reports.

As with all computerisation, it is necessary to ensure that the manual system works properly before attempting to computerise. A major problem is likely to be the shortage of skilled personnel to operate computerised systems, and such people may be in a position to defraud the system of large amounts. There must, therefore, be adequate arrangements for the supervision of the computerised system to avoid errors and fraud.

(For examples of improved local revenue performance, see Blore, Devas and Slater (2004), chapters 4 and 5.)

Note

1   In American textbooks, effectiveness is usually referred to as collection efficiency. We prefer to use the term effectiveness, since in normal usage efficiency is a measure of the resources consumed in achieving a specified objective (and that is the sense in which we use the term efficiency), whereas effectiveness is an indicator of how far the objective has been achieved.

References

Bird, R.M. and de Jantscher, M.C. (eds) (1992). *Improving Tax Administration in Developing Countries*. Geneva: International Monetary Fund.

Blore, I., Devas, N. and Slater, R. (2004). *Municipalities and Finance: A Sourcebook for Capacity Building*. London: Earthscan.

CHAPTER FOUR

Financing Capital Investment

....

Nick Devas

Sources of capital investment

Sub-national and local governments finance capital expenditure in various ways:

- Charges for the service concerned

- Budget surplus (i.e. recurrent revenues less recurrent expenditures)

- Government grants

- Sales of assets

- Borrowing

- Bond issues

- Community contributions/self-help

- Private investment and public-private partnerships.

Purposes of borrowing by sub-national and local governments

a) To fund short-term cash short-falls: A common practice, resulting from the uneven pattern of local government revenues and expenditures. This is usually financed through bank overdrafts (in the UK and other developed countries, it may also be financed by exchanges between authorities or short-term deposits from the public).

b) To finance investment which will generate income ('self-liquidating' projects), for example, for water supplies, markets, etc.

c) To finance capital development, including plant and machinery, which will not generate income directly: Practices vary widely, with the majority of such development being financed by loans in the UK (but less so than in the past), the USA and India. In most European countries, the bulk of capital investment is financed from current revenue.

d) To finance deficits in the annual recurrent budget: This is generally not permitted at local level (unlike at national level), but New York was a celebrated case, and the practice of 'creative accounting' disguised deficit financing in certain UK authorities in the 1980s. Deficit financing by default occurs in many local governments in the developing world, with shortfalls in forecasted revenues and the failure to clear short-term overdrafts (e.g. some Indian states and many local authorities in Kenya).

Arguments for and against borrowing by local governments

Borrowing by local governments for long- or medium-term development projects (e.g. infrastructure, buildings, plant and machinery) can be justified on the following grounds.

a) It can accelerate development, since borrowing permits a level of investment which is not limited by current fiscal capacity.

b) Such development may, in turn, generate increased local revenues, albeit indirectly, thus increasing the authority's financial capacity in the future; this is comparable to the private sector's borrowing to finance investment that will generate a profit.

c) It is fair, on the benefit principle of equity, that future generations, who will benefit from the investment, should contribute to the costs through loan repayments.

In addition, in certain circumstances, e.g. where the rate of inflation exceeds the rate of interest, it may be cheaper to borrow than to finance out of current revenue. However, such circumstances are rare and usually short-lived, and so do not provide a general justification for borrowing.

The arguments against borrowing by local governments are that:

a) Accountability and financial discipline may be weakened if local taxpayers are not faced immediately with the full cost of the development expenditure;

b) Excessive borrowing can build up an intolerable burden of debt-servicing in the future;

c) Public sector borrowing may contribute to inflation, through expansion of the money supply;

d) Public sector borrowing may attract scarce resources from 'productive' sectors (e.g. commerce, industry or agriculture), to the detriment of economic growth – the 'crowding out' argument.

Sources and methods of borrowing

There are a number of possible sources of loan finance for local governments:

a) Loans from central government;

b) Loans from international agencies, e.g. the World Bank, the African and Asian Development Banks or bilateral donors, usually channelled through central government;

c) Loans from a central credit institution or a loans fund for local authorities (see section on municipal credit institutions);

d) Loans or overdrafts from the local authority's bankers;

e) Direct borrowing from the public or the money market, e.g. by issuing local authority bonds (see section on municipal bonds);

f) Internal borrowing from reserve funds, e.g. superannuation funds and funds for renewal of plant and machinery;

g) Borrowing from other authorities (but usually only for short-term loans);

h) Hire purchase or leasing arrangements with equipment suppliers, or contractor finance for construction projects (while not strictly borrowing, the financial implications are much the same – a commitment to pay over a period).

Loan terms

Duration: The duration of a loan depends on its purpose. It may be just overnight for cash-flow requirements or 60 years for a building. Ideally, loan duration should be related to the life expectancy of the asset created. Many sub-national governments in developed countries operate consolidated funds, which borrow wholesale from the market for all purposes and then 'lend out' funds to individual projects on terms appropriate to that project, and which 'average out' the portfolio of repayment terms. Most international lenders want to 'roll over' their loans as quickly as possible, so longer-term finance may be hard to obtain, but central government 'consolidation' arrangements may be able to overcome this problem.

Interest rates: In a developed economy, interest rates are competitively determined, with differences in rates reflecting duration and relative perceived risks. In many developing and transitional economies, capital markets may be highly imperfect, with high interest rates reflecting the shortage of loanable funds. Attempts by governments to 'hold down' interest rates may be counter-productive, resulting in a drying up of loanable funds. High interest rates may also be a reflection of inflation; real interest rates are the difference between nominal interest rates and the anticipated rate of inflation.

Borrowing from internal sources (e.g. pensions or plant renewal funds) should be at a 'proper' rate of interest, i.e. one that reflects the interest that could be obtained from bank deposits or alternative investments with equivalent risks, to ensure that these funds are not decapitalised.

Grace periods: Loan terms may incorporate grace periods while construction is carried out, but interest is still payable during grace periods (although it may be added to amortisation payments following the grace period). For local governments in many countries, governments (and/or donors) may be the only source of loan finance, and so there may be little choice about terms, or even about the type of project.

Security: The relative security of loans to local governments may mean that terms are softer than they would be to riskier borrowers (although in some countries, defaults by local governments have made such lending much higher risk). Lenders normally require some specific security, such as:

- Collateral: the right to foreclose on the local government's assets (e.g. land, buildings or equipment);

- A lien over certain current revenues (e.g. revenues from a market constructed with a loan);

- A guarantee from the central government.

Where the lender is the government or a government institution, the simplest method of security is a lien over future grant payments to the local government, which can then be deducted at source. However, such arrangements reduce the risk to the lender, leading to 'moral hazard' and the risk of excessive lending (since the lender is sure of being repaid). Meanwhile, local taxpayers bear the burden as the flow of transfers is diverted to repay the loans. Government guarantees on loans are also undesirable, since they create a contingent liability on government, and may encourage irresponsible borrowing by the local government.

Conditionality: Lenders, especially international finance institutions, may impose conditions, not just about the implementation of the project (e.g. international competitive tendering, reporting, etc.) but also about the policy towards the whole sector (e.g. pricing policy or target beneficiaries). Management and reporting requirements may also be onerous.

Approvals and scrutiny

Three levels of approval are normally required for borrowing:

- Formal resolution of the governing body of the local government (e.g. the council);

- Permission from the central government to borrow;

- Agreement by the lender.

Approval will be based on the following considerations:

- The technical and financial soundness of the project itself;

- The merits of the scheme and the relative priority of the project in local, regional and national development plans;

- The capacity of the local government to service the debt.

In addition, the central government will be concerned with the overall level of sub-national borrowing and its impact on macroeconomic management. Experience from

Latin America has shown that unrestricted borrowing by sub-national governments can have a serious impact on macroeconomic stability (Ahmad and Devarajan, 2005).

Projects to be financed from loans tend to be subject to a higher degree of technical and financial scrutiny than do projects financed out of the recurrent budget. However, there is no logical reason why this should be so, just because the method of financing is different. In particular, central governments can often, because of their control over loan finance, exert a disproportionate influence on those activities to be financed by loans.

Criteria for appraising a project

For an income-generating project, appraisal is a straightforward projection of costs and revenues (making due allowance for uncertainties in the forecasts), and a comparison of the internal rate of return with the market rate of interest (or opportunity cost of capital).

For projects that do not generate income directly, some form of cost-benefit analysis is required which compares alternative uses for the same capital resources, using an appropriate rate of discount (e.g. the rate of interest which will apply to the proposed loan). Anticipated generation of revenues indirectly (e.g. the increase in property tax revenues that result from the development) will be a factor, as will be increased recurrent costs that arise (e.g. for operation and maintenance).

Borrowing capacity

Lenders – central governments, as well as local governments themselves – need to be sure that a borrowing local government does not become overextended in its borrowing. There is no agreed standard for assessing a local government's ability to repay loans. For income-earning investments, the main consideration will be whether the project fully covers its costs, taking account of the willingness and ability of users/beneficiaries to pay the charges for the service, and with due adjustment for risks. For other projects, the most usual measure is the debt-service ratio (DSR).

Debt-service ratio

The debt-service ratio compares the debt service that arises from the project (i.e. repayments of principal plus interest) with the authority's anticipated revenues. There are certain problems with the calculation of a DSR:

- What revenues should be included in the denominator – all revenues, or only those which are 'uncommitted'?

- Should grants be included as part of revenue? This is the case in the UK and for Union loans to states in India, where grant revenues can be used to pay debt-service charges on the grounds that debt service is part of current expenditure.

- How should revenues be projected, since they can be expected to increase (both because of the project itself and because of inflation) by the time loan repayments are required? (But how certain are we of these increased revenues? Have revised tax and charge rates already been approved? In addition, recurrent costs for operation and maintenance may increase as a result of the project.)

- What is an acceptable ratio of debt service obligations to revenues?

In addition, there are problems in applying the DSR:

- High revenue figures may not imply an ability to service high levels of debt, since there may a high level of committed expenditure against those revenues;

- Projections of revenues and expenditures can be manipulated to show the desired result;

- Rigid application of a DSR rule may prevent good projects going ahead without preventing inappropriate borrowing.

Alternative indicators of loan service capacity

- The level of revenues above committed expenditures, and the trends of revenue

- The extent of reserves/balances

- The track record of repayments of past loans

- A more sophisticated analysis of the overall financial health of the authority.

In practice, the DSR is not a widely used measure. No debt-service ceiling is applied in the UK; in the USA, the normal practice of local authorities is to say that debt service should not exceed 20 per cent of an authority's current revenues.

Municipal credit institutions and development funds

Many countries have some form of central fund for lending to local authorities (El Daher, 2000). These may be known by various names – municipal credit institutions (MCIs) or municipal development funds (MDFs), and may be constituted in various ways (Davey, 1988):

- Instituted and directed by central government (e.g. the Public Works Loans Board in the UK);

- Instituted and subscribed by the local governments themselves (e.g. the Municipal Credit Bank in Belgium);

- Jointly owned and controlled by central and local governments (e.g. the Bank of the Netherlands Municipalities and FUNDACOMUN in Venezuela).

Capital may derive from various sources:

- From central government, in the form of grants, initial capitalisation, loans, deposited reserves, proceeds of a specific tax, etc.;

- From local authorities, through share capital, deposited reserves, pension funds, a share of the proceeds of a particular tax, etc.;

- From the capital market, through share capital, deposits from the public, issue of debentures, national savings bonds, premiums on national insurance, etc.;

- From international borrowing, whether commercial or from bilateral or multilateral agencies;

- From operating profits;

- From repayment of loans (a revolving fund).

Centralised loans funds have some advantages as a source of loan finance for local governments:

- For those with capital to invest, such funds offer a more accessible and more secure place to invest than an individual local government; they can offer a variety of investment arrangements (bonds, debentures, personal savings accounts, etc.) with different terms to suit different investors.

- The scale of their borrowing means that they may have greater flexibility in timing borrowing according to fluctuating market conditions. It also means that they can gain economies of scale and have access to greater financial expertise. Combined with the greater security, this means that funds can be acquired on better terms than local authorities could obtain individually.

- They are likely to have a better understanding of the needs of local governments than do commercial lending agencies, and can build up expertise in relevant types of project.

- They may be able to represent the needs and interests of local governments in external negotiations.

- They may also be able to provide common technical services for local governments, e.g. in project design and execution (such as FUNDACOMUN in Venezuela).

However, the experience of municipal loan funds in much of Africa has not been happy, with lending often at below market rates, so that repayments are eroded by inflation, and defaults on repayments. As a result, several such funds (e.g. in Kenya and Uganda) have been decapitalised and then wound up.

Municipal bonds

Municipal bonds are the main way in which local governments in the USA finance capital investment. In recent years, USAID has been 'selling' the idea of bonds in many developing and transitional countries. Bonds can work well for very large city or municipal governments that have some credibility in the capital market, and may give a greater sense of financial autonomy than borrowing through a MCI (although any borrowing is still likely to require central government approval). With municipal bonds, the risks remain with the private sector, rather than becoming a contingent liability on government.

However, municipal bonds have severe limitations, especially where capital markets are undeveloped. In such situations, it may be very difficult for an individual municipality to establish the creditworthiness necessary to float a bond. Since bond issuing normally requires a financial intermediary to underwrite the bond, this is little different from an MCI. In India, there have been some successful schemes for municipalities organised on a state-level basis, but these require quite a high level of government (or donor) intervention to make them work (Blore, Devas and Slater, 2004). The cost of bond issue can be very high.

One positive feature of municipal bonds in emerging capital markets is the development of credit-rating agencies. The detailed analysis which they make of a municipality's financial health may be considerably more rigorous than the central government's scrutiny of local government financial performance. It is said that in India this has resulted in considerably sharpened municipal financial management and reporting. However, the credit-rating process can be very expensive for local governments.

Alternative sources of investment funds

There are numerous other ways in which capital investment by local governments can be financed, including a variety of public-private partnerships:

a) *Asset sales:* Where a local government has surplus assets, e.g. land and buildings, these can be sold to finance new investment. It will be important that such asset sales are treated as capital income, so that the revenue is not used up in recurrent expenditure (a frequent problem in post-1990 local governments in central and eastern Europe).

b) *Private sector investment,* e.g. through a franchise, BOT (build-operate-transfer) or BOO (build-operate-own) arrangements. These have been widely used in south-east Asia to construct new infrastructure such as mass transit systems and highways. There remain questions about the cost-effectiveness of such arrangements (and the transparency of the tendering process in some cases).

c) *Leveraging:* The local government may put in a certain amount of capital, for example in land rehabilitation or basis infrastructure, in order to 'lever' a larger amount of private sector investment in new development. This model has been widely used in the UK for urban regeneration projects.

d) **Joint ventures**: For example, where the local government provides the land and the private sector provides the capital – again, widely used in the past in the UK for regeneration projects.

e) **Private finance initiative (PFI):** This is the UK name for a system whereby the central government or local government contracts with a private company to construct, maintain and operate a building such as a hospital or prison, with the government leasing the facility on an annual basis. (The public sector still provides the service within the facility.) The rules for PFI in the UK require the private sector to bear sufficient risk, i.e. the contract is not guaranteed over the long term. The main motivation for this model in the UK has been to reduce the public-sector borrowing requirement (PSBR), and some regard PFI as a form of 'creative accounting'. There remain significant questions about the relative costs and quality of PFI schemes.

f) **Leasing** of capital equipment, vehicles, etc., rather than purchasing, with the capital finance being provided by the private sector. This avoids having to borrow, and it offers flexibility, but long-term lease arrangements involve a payment obligation that can be regarded as the equivalent of loan repayment.

g) **Sale-and-leaseback** of municipal capital assets, in which assets are sold in order to release capital funds and then are leased back. This was used by some local governments in the UK in the 1980s as a way of avoiding stringent controls on borrowing (and was referred to as 'creative accounting'), but was subsequently made illegal.

h) **Community investment:** A common practice in developing countries is for communities to undertake the construction of facilities such as schools, health clinics and rural roads, with or without some funding from local or central government. While this can greatly reduce the capital costs for the local government, it may mean imposing a burden on poor communities while better off neighbourhoods benefit from facilities provided in the past by the public sector.

References

Ahmad, J. and Devarajan, S. (2005). 'Decentralization and Service Delivery', World Bank Research Working Paper 3603. Washington, DC: World Bank.

Blore, I., Devas, N. and Slater, R. (2004). *Municipalities and Finance: A Sourcebook for Capacity Building*. London: Earthscan.

Davey, K.J. (1988). *Municipal Development Funds and Intermediaries*. Washington, DC: World Bank.

El Daher, S. (2000). *Specialized Financial Intermediaries for Local Governments: A Market-Based Tool for Local Infrastructure Finance*. Washington, DC: World Bank.

CHAPTER FIVE

Innovative Approaches to Municipal Infrastructure Financing

Pritha Venkatachalam

Introduction

The twin dilemma of what constitutes adequate local government financing and how to mobilise it has confounded academics and practitioners alike. Typically, only immobile tax bases, such as property taxes, are assigned to local jurisdictions. Borrowing at the local level has not found favour, especially in developing countries, as the traditional thesis of capital financing professed that local government borrowing is irresponsible and should be subject to considerable restrictions.

However, these conventional theories have been challenged by the recent trends of urbanisation and globalisation, which have heightened pressure on cities' growth and infrastructure. Simultaneously, political decentralisation strategies have pushed downwards the responsibility for coping with the explosive demand for urban services. Given that immobile local revenues cannot be expanded infinitely, strengthening conventional sources of municipal income promises, at best, to cover the revenue expenditures of local governments or to provide an insignificant surplus for capital expenses. In this scenario of growing vertical fiscal imbalance between function and finance, government grants and donor funds have proved inadequate to meet local capital spending. Hence, central governments are gradually embracing the idea of local governments accessing private finance for investments in public infrastructure and services. Since private equity, encumbered by dividend expectations, is generally more expensive and difficult to raise, debt is preferred to bridge the fiscal gap.

The typical options for infrastructure debt financing are borrowing from financial institutions and development banks, accessing capital markets or soliciting private sector participation through contracts, leases and concessions. However, basic urban services like water supply and sanitation, sewerage and solid waste management are unattractive to private financiers, given their characteristics of time and space externalities, limited cost recovery, high risk and long gestation. Also, in the context of developing countries, typically only limited liquidity and financial products are available. In addition, loans from banks and financial institutions are usually of shorter tenure – 5–7 years – and may require sovereign guarantees. Hence, many developing countries are trying to develop domestic and international capital markets to mobilise private savings for urban infrastructure involving lengthier payback periods.

India, with its large capital markets, is also experimenting with sub-national debt in some states. The southern state of Tamil Nadu has been hailed as a forerunner in innovative market-based financing of urban infrastructure (IADF, 2004: 3; Kehew et al., 2005). This chapter aims to evaluate the urban financing techniques adopted in Tamil Nadu, with a view to examining whether and to what extent they have facilitated 'municipal debt market development'. A few isolated instances of capital market access do not constitute a credit market, which involves the development of a long-term viable option for capital financing. A municipal debt market is a system with a variety of local borrowers and lenders, where credit allocations are based on pricing decisions that balance demand and supply factors. As an economy grows and financial needs increase, these markets serve to integrate sub-national demand for investment capital with the supply of funds (Freire et al., 2004).

This chapter is divided into four sections. The next section is a brief summary of international experiences in market-based local borrowing. The following two sections describe the innovative urban financing approaches adopted in Tamil Nadu, and assess whether these innovations facilitate long-term market development. Finally, the chapter concludes that Tamil Nadu has spearheaded the advance of municipal debt instruments and stimulated nascent sub-national debt markets in India. But in order for these financial accomplishments to be translated into enduring local bond markets, they need to be complemented by corresponding project development capabilities in urban local governments, without which the funds borrowed cannot be fruitfully invested.

International experiences

While most developing and transition countries are intensifying their thrust to develop vigorous local credit markets to support decentralisation initiatives, sub-national governments in North America and Western Europe have a long history of harnessing private debt to build urban infrastructure. However, the credit models championed in these regions are instructive in their diversity: while North America relies mainly on municipal bonds, Western Europe has developed home-grown development banks, and emerging markets are attempting to establish one of these models or a hybrid, either directly or through specialised financial intermediaries (Peterson, 2003).

The US municipal bond market was created to cater for the urban boom of the 1850s. Today it is the most sophisticated in terms of its depth and ability to finance the long-term cash flow needs of municipalities across different sectors of urban development (Temel, 2001: 49; Johnson, 2004). Specific purpose revenue bonds have matured into the primary source of funding for capital projects, but general obligation bonds issued against the surety of local government revenues are also prevalent. The Federal Government has endorsed decentralised financing by conferring tax-free status on municipal bonds, and contributing to state revolving funds and bond banks. These intermediaries pool the borrowing needs of marginal local entities that are unable to access capital markets on their own (El-Daher, 1997: 1–3). A mature federal system comprising strong sub-national governments, matched with an enabling investment environment, has promoted the growth of US municipal debt markets.

Western Europe, on the other hand, leveraged its historic preferential access to long-term saving deposits and government contributions to establish municipal banks and financial institutions. Development municipal banks like Crédit Local de France, BNG of the Netherlands, Banco de Credito of Spain, and Crédit Communal Belgique of Belgium handle various bundled services such as credit evaluation and project monitoring for municipal infrastructure projects prepared by local governments. With financial deregulation, these banks are also converging into the competitive capital markets to raise funds (Peterson, 1996: 32–34; El-Daher, 2000: 2).

Despite the backing of international agencies and national authorities in creating municipal development funds in emerging markets, developing self-sustaining local credit markets has proved challenging. The pioneering MDF in Brazil provides loans to municipalities and special utility companies and has enjoyed over 30 years of commendable loan recovery rates and less than 5 per cent non-performing loans (Peterson, 2003: 12). South African local governments have a legacy of self-reliance and sophisticated municipal bond markets. The Infrastructure Finance Corporation Limited in South Africa also provides loans to municipalities and other statutory boards and utilities. Similarly, Vietnam has recently established provincial local development investment funds under state ownership, in order to develop infrastructure and enable the mobilisation of private capital and its participation in local government projects.

Zimbabwe has chosen the safe path of issuing municipal bonds with sovereign guarantees, thereby not relying on the prudence of local borrowers (Phelps, 1997: 99). Low domestic savings have motivated some cities like Sofia in Bulgaria, and Moscow and St Petersburg in Russia, to float foreign bonds (Marfitsin et al., 1997: 80; Epstein et al., 2000: 89).

The other successful model has been that of a contingent financier, which provides products such as guarantees or insurance that are contingent to the main project financing. FINDETER in Colombia, established in 1989 as a second tier government financial intermediary, rediscounts bank loans to local borrowers. It has motivated commercial banks to be responsible for municipal credit risks across sectors such as transportation, water and sewerage, and education. FINDETER is financially and institutionally viable, and has recently diversified its client portfolio to include departmental and municipal service companies. The latest development in its active municipal credit system is the graduation of larger cities like Bogotá from bank loans to bonds (Kehew et al., 2005: 20–26; Peterson, 2000: 33). The Czech Republic presents another example of a diversified municipal debt market, characterised by a mix of municipal bonds issued by almost all the country's large cities and commercial bank loans with extended tenure. Such competitive lengthening of loan periods from 8 to 15 years is made feasible by the Municipal Infrastructure Finance Program (MUFIS), an MDF that provides long duration loans to banks for on-lending to local governments (Matoušková et al., 1997: 7–16). The third such example is the Local Government Unit Guarantee Corporation (LGUGC) in the Philippines. Initiated as the brain-child of the Department of Finance in 1997, LGUGC provides insurance to municipal investors. It is uniquely structured as a jointly owned public-private entity, supplemented by a 30 per cent USAID-backed credit guarantee. It has also instituted a proprietary credit rating system to identify creditworthy issuers. Injecting liquidity into the dormant municipal bond market, it has offered local bodies a cheaper alternative to loans from government financial institutions (USAID, 1997: 5; Orial, 2003: 405–410).

The above summary indicates that no decentralised municipal system is dependent on a single borrowing option for all its infrastructure needs. While many governments have instituted MDFs to front-end inexperienced local borrowers, the more successful cases, like Colombia and the Czech Republic, have matured into a multitiered municipal credit system. Larger creditworthy local entities access cheaper bond finances against their own balance sheet, while small and medium entities continue to leverage financial intermediaries, development banks and government grants. Nevertheless, as has been experienced in some countries with success in bond financing, the preference for bonds for debt financing is chiefly because of their longer tenure and lower cost, where a high credit rating can be secured. Most often, a line of credit from international financial institutions has proved instrumental in extending the maturities of local debt instruments. However, the key to financial independence is to move gradually from donor support to own or market-raised funds, which demands capable local units that can attract private investors.

Innovative municipal financing in Tamil Nadu

The need for capital market financing

India's constitution ordains that it is a union of states and union territories, with residual legislative powers vested in the central government. Despite the existence of urban local bodies (ULBs) even prior to British colonisation, the status of 'democratic institutions of self government' was not formally conferred on them until 1992, with the passing of the Constitution (Seventy-fourth Amendment) Act. This landmark amendment provided for direct elections to the three types of municipalities: town *panchayats* in communities in transition from rural to urban areas; municipal councils for small urban areas; and municipal corporations for larger urban areas. It also proposed the formation of state finance commissions (SFCs) every five years, to recommend principles to strengthen municipal finances through assigned taxes, devolved taxes and grants in aid from the state.[1]

Prior to the 1990s, Tamil Nadu oscillated between decentralisation and recentralisation of power over ULBs, with irregular municipal elections and wide fluctuations in fiscal devolution (Guhan, 1986: 34). However, after the 1992 Amendment, Tamil Nadu has led India's decentralisation efforts. It passed the conformity legislation in 1994, conducted two rounds of local government elections, and constituted and implemented the recommendations of the SFCs in 1996 and 2001 (Mukundan, 2005: 2).

The state ULBs comprise six municipal corporations and 151 municipalities, including 49 town *panchayats* which were upgraded to third grade municipalities in June 2004.[2] Urban areas with a population over 500,000 and an average annual income for the last three years of over Rs 300 million are classified as municipal corporations, and those with populations of over 30,000 and income over Rs 5 million as municipalities.[3]

Tamil Nadu is the one of most urbanised states of India with an urban population of 27.5 million, about 44 per cent of the state population.[4] The average annual growth rate of the urban population from 1991 to 2001 was approximately 4.2 per cent. While Tamil Nadu's capital, Chennai, is its largest city (with a population of 4.4 million), unlike other Indian states, its urban population is distributed over various types of urban agglomerations and towns.[5]

Such rapid urbanisation has imposed an added strain on existing infrastructure deficiencies in the state. However, the Government of Tamil Nadu (GoTN) has substantially increased financial devolution to local bodies on the recommendation of the SFCs. This has allowed the ULBs to maintain operating surpluses on their revenue account (Table 5.1). In addition, capital investments post-devolution have grown substantially year on year, with the exception of 2000–2002, when the state government faced severe fiscal deficits (Table 5.2).[6]

Table 5.1. Revenue accounts of all ULBs, 1998–2003 (Rs million)

Category	1998–99	1999–2000	2000–01	2001–02	2002–03
Own and other revenues	7,037	8,537	10,944	10,646	11,758
Assigned revenue and devolutions	5,590	6,423	6,109	4,429	8,953
Total revenues	12,627	14,960	17,053	15,174	20,711
Total revenue expenditure	8.914	10,405	11,808	11,892	14,896
Revenue surplus/deficit	3,713	4,555	5,245	3,282	5,815

Source: *Twelfth Finance Commission Report 2005–10*, p. 443

Table 5.2. Capital investments across ULBs in Tamil Nadu, 1995–2003 (Rs million)

All ULBs	Pre-devolution				Post-devolution			
	1995–96	1996–97	1997–98	1998–99	1999–2000	2000–01	2001–02	2002–03
Capital investments	2,073	2,380	4,056	5,570	6,337	6,163	4,985	6,598

Source: *Twelfth Finance Commission Report 2005–10*, p. 443; *Second State Finance Commission Report 2001*, p. 44

Despite such heartening fiscal developments, Tamil Nadu still falls far short of its requisite capital investment. The capital financing estimates of the second SFC indicate that the total infrastructure needs of ULBs projected for the period 2002–2007 are over *three times* in excess of the optimum investment capability from self-raised revenues and devolutions (Table 5.3). An analysis of infrastructure requirements by sector indicates that water supply and sanitation, roads and storm water drains are the areas most in need of investment.[7]

Table 5.3. Financing gap for infrastructure investments in Tamil Nadu (Rs million)

Category	2002–2007	
	Investment required as per norms	Optimum investment capability
Municipal corporations	22.55	9.75
Municipalities	26.79	6.50
Town *panchayats*[a]	29.70	8.03
Total	79.04	24.28

[a]Includes the 611 former town *panchayats* before the 2004 Government Order
Source: *Second State Finance Commission Report 2001*, pp. 52–63

The shortfall in essential infrastructure financing provides a strong motivation for the state to explore alternative sources of capital to supplement existing local revenues. A range of financial innovations have been pursued, including the mobilisation of funds through a unique private-public financial intermediary model, capital market access using customised credit enhancements and ingenious pooled financing of a project portfolio of smaller local bodies. These have been accompanied by far-reaching reforms in municipal accounting, automation and e-governance, and performance management systems.

Tamil Nadu Urban Development Fund

The Tamil Nadu Urban Development Fund (TNUDF) was promoted in 1996, essentially a make-over of the previous state-owned and operated municipal urban development fund (MUDF) created in 1988. All assets and liabilities of the MUDF were transferred to the TNUDF, which was incorporated as a trust by GoTN with a Rs 1.2 billion capital contribution. By 2000–2001, the fund had grown to Rs 2 billion, with 29 per cent of its capital invested by three leading all-India financial institutions – the Industrial Credit and Investment Corporation of India, Housing Development Finance Corporation and Infrastructure Leasing and Financial Services, and a reduced 71 per cent equity participation by GoTN. Tamil Nadu Urban Infrastructure Financial Services Limited (TNUIFSL) was established as the fund's asset management company. It had a majority private stake, with the same three financial institutions holding 51 per cent equity and GoTN contributing 49 per cent. The TNUDF was thus India's first public-private financial intermediary managed by a predominantly private fund manager, geared to mobilising long-term debt for municipal infrastructure (Pradhan 2003: 131).[8] In a little over a year of operation, the TNUDF approved municipal loans worth Rs 1.5 billion, compared to MUDF's sanction of Rs 2 billion over eight years (World Bank, 2005: 3).

In addition to equity, the fund had access to a line of credit of about Rs 3.7 billion (US$80 million) from the World Bank, on-lent by GoTN (World Bank, 1999: 25). Leveraging its public-private capital base, the TNUDF ventured to raise cheaper debt funds by floating five years non-convertible bonds in November 2000. The issue of Rs 1000 million was offered on private placement. Despite being the maiden non-guaranteed bond issue by an MDF in India,[9] it reaped an oversubscription of Rs 1,100.5 million. Various commercial banks purchased 70.5 per cent of the bonds, TNUDF contributors 12 per cent, regional rural banks 9.5 per cent and insurance companies 8 per cent (Kehew et al., 2005: 29).

Designed as neither a general obligation (pledged on overall municipality revenues) nor a revenue bond (pledged on specific project revenues) as evolved in the USA, the credit instrument was indigenously conceptualised as a structured debt obligation, with a dedicated escrow of reliable income sources. A bond service fund (BSF), equivalent to one year's principal and interest, was maintained as collateral until expiry of the bonds. These proceeds were safely invested in best-rated liquid securities like Government of India Treasury bills. The debt obligation was accorded seniority status and ranked first in the pecking order for repayment. In the eventuality of drawing down the BSF, the TNUDF provided the additional cushion of an escrow on its own current account, which would be frozen for withdrawals until the BSF was replenished. Such an elaborate credit enhancement mechanism was intended to protect the debt from adverse political factors and duly obtained a 'high credit quality/low credit risk' rating from the Indian Credit Rating Agency.[10] The high safety rating enabled a competitive coupon rate of 11.85 per cent per annum, less than 1 per cent premium over the comparable government security rate of 11 per cent.[11]

The TNUDF spearheaded significant growth in fresh asset creation across ULBs. As of 31 March 2001, its total assets were worth Rs 6.6 billion, comprised chiefly of loans to ULBs (71 per cent); the remainder included investments and current assets.[12] The core beneficiaries were smaller municipalities and town *panchayats* facing a sizeable backlog of essential infrastructure investments. Over 175 projects were sanctioned by March 2002, primarily for roads and bridges, sewerage and sanitation, and water supply, but also some commercial projects. By March 2004, the portfolio consisted of a larger proportion of sewerage and water supply projects, resulting from TNUDF assistance to the National River Conservation Project, which preserved state waterways from being polluted by the overflow of sewage (Table 5.4).[13]

Table 5.4. TNUDF project portfolio by sector – loans sanctioned

Sector	March 2002		March 2004	
	Amount (Rs million)	%	Amount (Rs million)	%
Bridges and roads	2,853.40	65	2,929.7	48
Sewerage and sanitation	971.40	22	2,285.1	38
Water supply	267.00	6	506.5	8
Bus stations and commercial complexes	215.70	5	215.7	4
Storm water drains	56.30	1	56.3	1
Miscellaneous	54.70	1	54.9	1
Total	4,418.50	100	6,048.2	100

Source: *TNUDF Activity Reports*, 2001–2002 and 2003–2004

The TNUDF resourcefully bagged a series of 'firsts' through the inventive structuring of projects financed, notably for the smaller and infrastructurally backward local bodies. The Fund facilitated the first toll bridge on a build-operate-transfer contract in Karur Municipality at an estimated cost of Rs 160 million. This mandated a regulatory amendment of the Tamil Nadu State Toll Act to authorise a ULB to sign a BOT contract. Another first was a build-own-operate-transfer sewerage network for Alandur Municipality designed to meet future projections of a population of 300,000 persons in 2027, at a cost of Rs 480 million. The municipality had only waterborne sanitation facilities decanting into open storm water drains, precipitating unsanitary conditions. The debt burden for the sewerage system was resourcefully mitigated through one-time connection deposits paid by beneficiaries. The deposit amount was collectively determined through detailed consultations with the local population over many months. These finally concluded in a tiered contribution structure with households paying Rs 5,000 per connection, cross-subsidised by industrial and commercial establishments which contributed Rs 10,000 (Mathur, 2002: 226–28).[14] Willing deposit payments for public infrastructure had no precedent in India and laid the foundation for a commercial mind-set to such projects. A third project was the construction of bus stands for Tirunelveli Municipal Corporation, where the TNUDF loan was fully repaid with cash payments from potential users. The complex recouped an annual saving of Rs 2.5 million by outsourcing operation and maintenance to a private contractor (World Bank, 2005: 8).

The TNUDF also built a financial track record of timely loan recovery. For loans appraised by the TNUDF, the terms of agreement established escrows of ULB tax and non-tax collections. In addition to these safeguards, TNUIFSL, the fund manager, initiated constant follow-up of undue delays in repayment. Periodic reviews of the arrears portfolio ensured record recovery rates, consistently above 99 per cent.[15]

The strong loan portfolio held by the TNUDF was the result of emphasis on stringent qualification criteria for both the project and the borrower. These included sector specification, borrower eligibility criteria, minimum financial and economic rates of return, and environmental and social safeguards (Sood, 2004: 430–31).

Once selected, ULBs were eligible not only for TNUDF loans but also two grant funds from GoTN for poverty alleviation and technical assistance for project development/preparation, also operated and managed by the TNUIFSL.

These initiatives were also instrumental in sparking sustained reforms in the overall administration and management of ULBs. Tamil Nadu is the first and only state in India to have moved from cash-based accounting to double entry accrual accounting across all municipal corporations and municipalities by April 2000. The ULBs have also computerised all their accounts and registration records, improving efficiency of collections and increasing information transparency (Joshi, 2004: 344–46). Tamil Nadu has developed a state-wide urban performance indicators system to compare service levels, operational and management efficiency, and financial performance across ULBs. The first such comparative assessment of ULB performance was undertaken with the data collected by the first SFC, and informed planning and policy-making in the state (FIRE, 1999a: 1–3).

Water and Sanitation Pooled Fund

In order to ensure the inclusion of weaker ULBs and relatively small but essential projects, GoTN instituted a special purpose vehicle called the Water and Sanitation Pooled Fund (WSPF) in August 2002. Incorporated as a trust with a contribution of only Rs 10,000 from GoTN, the idea was to reduce the transaction costs of market access for the smaller local entities. The WSPF was a thinly funded, leveraged structure that would not impose high dividend costs on beneficiaries.[16] This fund was also managed by the TNUIFSL (see Figure 5.1).

Pooling the water and sanitation requirements of 13 municipalities and town *panchayats*, the WSPF mobilised capital market finances through an unsecured structured debt obligation for Rs 304.1 million in December 2002. Based on the principle of credit aggregation, this was the first successful pooled market financing outside the USA. It proposed to upgrade the bond rating of a judicious mix of financially strong and weak ULBs and achieve economies of scale for small city projects which could not individually access capital markets (Johnson, 2004). Issued for 15 years tenure, it is the only truly long-term municipal infrastructure bond in India.[17] Beyond a plain vanilla issue, the structured financing was enriched with put and call options after ten years. The options provide a safety net to investors who may wish to divest their holding before maturity, thereby increasing bond liquidity (Leigland, 1997: 8).

In order to bolster market confidence in India's maiden pooled bond, the debt nestled in multiple layers of credit enhancements such as a no-lien escrow account established by the 13 ULBs on all their revenues, a BSF of Rs 69 million, invested in low-risk liquid securities, and guarantees from the USAID development credit authority guarantee and GoTN.[18] The enhanced pooled debt instrument secured a dual 'high safety' credit rating from Fitch Ratings and the Indian Credit Rating Agency. Privately placed at a competitive rate of 9.2 per cent,[19] it was immediately subscribed for by commercial banks and provident funds (FIRE, 2003:2–3).

The bond proceeds were lent back-to-back to the 13 ULBs in the pool at 9.2 per cent per annum, resulting in substantial savings versus their individual borrowing rate of 12 per cent (Ghodke, 2004: 145). The shortlisted portfolio included water supply augmentation schemes for eight municipalities and town *panchayats* adjacent to Chennai plus five other municipalities, and an underground drainage project for Madurai Corporation (Table 5.5). A special characteristic of these projects was that they were all fully or nearly completed and most of them were already financed by the TNUDF. Structurally, the credit enhancement mechanisms aimed to overcome liquidity and political risks, and the project completion aspect surmounted development risk so that the funds could be deployed immediately.[20]

Table 5.5. Pooled finance bond projects

S. No.		Urban local body	Proceeds of bond	
			Rs million	%
		Water supply schemes		
1		Ambattur Municipality	6.7	2
2		Tambaram Municipality	10.9	4
3		Madhavaram Municipality	19.4	6
4		Rajapalayam Municipality	5.1	2
		Adjacent urban areas (AUA)		
5	(i)	Alandur Municipality	40.3	13
6	(ii)	Pammal Town *Panchayat*	35.7	12
7	(iii)	Ankapathur Town *Panchayat*	17.8	6
8	(iv)	Ullagaram Town *Panchayat*	28.1	9
9	(v)	Porur Town *Panchayat*	54.7	18
10	(vi)	Maduravoyal Town *Panchayat*	13.8	5
11	(vii)	Valsaravakkam Town *Panchayat*	17.9	6
12	(viii)	Meenambakkam Town *Panchayat*	1.6	1
		Underground drainage		
13		Madurai Corporation	52.0	17
		Total	304.1	100

Source: Memorandum of private placement for non-convertible redeemable bonds issued by WSPF, 2002

Figure 5.1. Municipal development funds framework in Tamil Nadu

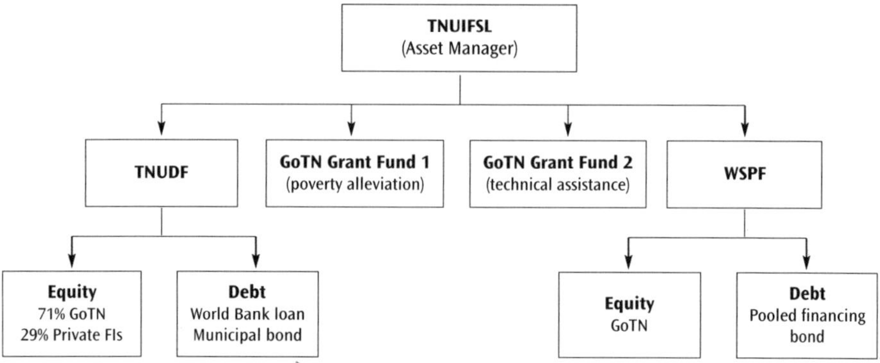

Following these successful bond issues spearheaded by the municipal funds TNUDF and WSPF, there have been several other instances of successful capital market access by municipalities and infrastructure entities in the state.

Assessment of municipal bond 'market development'

The moot question is whether the instances of innovative financing arrangements and capital market relationships described here have been successful in developing long-term municipal bond markets in Tamil Nadu. Whereas in developed markets, the introduction of new financing instruments such as municipal bonds may demand research, marketing and perhaps legislative changes, their establishment in emerging markets may necessitate the development of elements of the market itself, on both the demand and supply sides (Phelps, 1997: 5). The demand side represents the financial, technical and administrative capabilities of ULBs as borrowers, and the supply side denotes capital market or lenders' characteristics. To create lasting credit markets, these twin forces need to be developed in parallel, so that the finances borrowed can be optimally utilised.

Tamil Nadu has certainly achieved many supply-side successes through its financial innovations. However, as already mentioned, the foundation of municipal bond markets requires robust supply- and demand-side elements, and financial structuring represents only supply-side improvements (Figure 5.2).

As the USA is the pioneer and leader in municipal infrastructure bonds, its characteristics have become the yardstick for donors and governments evaluating emerging market funds (Leigland, 1997: 2). Yet the US model may not prove ideal for the assessment of municipal credit markets in developing countries. As witnessed in most coun-

Figure 5.2. Illustrative municipal bond model in Tamil Nadu

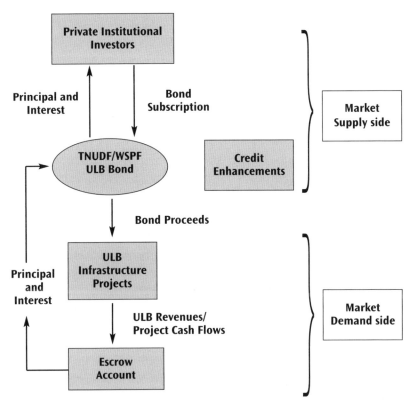

tries, despite strong financial indicators, the MDFs did not succeed in developing private debt markets owing to low investor confidence in ULB performance. On the contrary, local governments in the USA have strong financial, technical and administrative capabilities. Additionally, there is a retail pull from private savers to invest in municipal growth (Ghodke, 2004: 145). Hence, the role of a US financial intermediary is restricted to sourcing the cheapest capital funds on best possible terms (Peterson, 1996: 18). Imposing the US prototype with its robust demand-side factors onto developing countries leads to an excessive preoccupation with the financial aspects of market development at the cost of insufficient investment in local government capacities.

In developing countries, demand-side strengthening involves building the financial viability of local bodies, as well as their skills in project development and execution. As expressed by Peterson (1998: 1), 'creditworthiness of municipalities is at the heart of borrowing'. Justifiably, there has been enormous focus on fortifying the revenue base of ULBs in Tamil Nadu through streamlining their tax and non-tax revenues, increasing financial devolution and obtaining state government guarantees where possible.

The weak link in Tamil Nadu's market development pursuits is the demand-side capability of preparation and structuring of capital investment programmes. Temporal synchronisation between a fund's mobilisation and its productive deployment is often overlooked in debt financing. Nonetheless, if a timelag ensues between the bond issue and project readiness, the costs of capital market financing can outweigh the potential benefits. Municipal bonds in Tamil Nadu were all issued at or above market yields and most of them were taxed. In a decreasing interest rate regime, if project preparation is tardy, investment of idle bond proceeds presents negative arbitrage opportunities. This was also evinced in the debt financing of Ahmedabad Municipal Corporation in Gujarat, the first ULB in India to float a non-guaranteed public bond. Lack of specialised project preparation support and delays in the approval process led to bond funds remaining unused for two years. Worse still, because of falling interest rates, the returns earned on investing these unused funds were lower than the interest payable on the bonds (FIRE, 2001: 3–4).

The other weak link is the limited municipal staff who may not possess the resources and talent to manage all aspects of asset creation and service delivery in the local area. Additionally, project development for private sector funding is more demanding than government grants. Besides the technical design aspect, financial project planning needs to match the rigour that capital market borrowing imposes. This necessitates projects that are commercially viable with suitable risk mitigation structures, such as having access to other dedicated revenue sources (FIRE, 1999b: 1). It is generally accepted, on poverty alleviation and affordability grounds, that grants or subsidies are required to reduce the loan burden for basic infrastructural investments. Nevertheless, the project should be structured to at least recover the debt component.

In sum, the real binding constraints in long-term municipal market development in Tamil Nadu are not financial bottlenecks, as popularly perceived, but ULB capacity to structure and execute viable projects and contain development risks. In order for ULBs to graduate from concessionary to market finance, they need to broaden their technical and financial skills and resources.

Conclusion

Many local governments have resorted to private financing of public infrastructure under the pressures of urbanisation and fiscal stress. Experiments have ranged from Western models of municipal bonds and development banks, to local municipal development funds, often assisted by donors. While most trials can claim success for some instances of capital market access, the overall track record in developing long-term municipal credit markets has proved rather dismal. Devoid of market development, the issue of bonds will remain sporadic and an unsustainable basis of capital financing.

The Indian state of Tamil Nadu has been lauded as a progressive example of capital market borrowing. Nevertheless, unless local governments develop demand-side capabilities in project preparation and development, financial innovations will be unable to build durable municipal bond markets. The seeds sowed for market creation can grow only if both demand- and supply-side factors are developed in tandem, so that the debt funds mobilised are deployed promptly in productive projects.

Tamil Nadu has accomplished a series of financial innovations. It shored up nearly Rs 3000 million within five years through a series of pioneering issues such as India's first bond issued by a joint private-public municipal fund, India's first revenue bond, and the world's first pooled financing bond outside the USA. From a supply-side perspective, Tamil Nadu's ingenious financial engineering overcame potential credit risks and successfully secured private institutional finance, even for non-remunerative infrastructure in small towns.

However, credit enhancements do not cover development and construction risks, which depend on the demand-side strengths of local governments in structuring and executing projects on time. The cost of market financing will grow disproportionately if funds mobilised are forced into lower interest-bearing investments because of a time-lag in project readiness. In addition, in the absence of self-reliance in financial and project appraisal skills, ULBs will be unable to secure the best financial terms available in the market. As is held by theorists of decentralisation, devolution of functions should be followed by the devolution of finance and functionaries (Subrahmanyam and Choudhury, 2004: 20).

The financial experiments of Tamil Nadu are currently being extended across other states of India, as well as across other emerging markets. In the race to crowd in private funds, donors and governments should be careful that they do not crowd out vital local government capabilities.

Notes

1   The Constitution (Seventy-fourth Amendment) Act, 1992.
2   *Tamil Nadu Government Gazette*, No. 149/G.O. No. 270, June 2004; *Tamil Nadu Government Gazette*, No. 150/Ordinance No. 7, June 2004. Until June 2004, there were 611 town panchayats, of which 562 were reclassified as special village panchayats and 49 were upgraded to third grade municipalities by government order.
3   Tamil Nadu District Municipalities Act 1920, Section 4.
4   Census of India, 2001. The all-India average urban population (2001) is 26 per cent.
5   Census of Tamil Nadu, 2001.
6   *Twelfth Finance Commission Report 2005–2010*, p. 443; *Second State Finance Commission Report 2002–2007*, p. 44.
7   *Second State Finance Commission Report 2002–2007*, pp. 52–63,
8   *Financial Review of TNUDF*, 2005, pp. 3, 7.
9   Individual municipal corporations like Bangalore Corporation and Ahmedabad Corporation had issued bonds prior to 2000.
10 ICRA (2000). ICRA credit rating rationale on Tamil Nadu Urban Development Fund Bond issue.

11 TNUDF Annual Accounts, 31 March 2002; RBI (2000), 'Selected economic indicators', *Reserve Bank of India Bulletin*, November 2000.
12 TNUDF Annual Accounts, 31 March 2001.
13 TNUDF Activity Reports 2001–2002 and 2003–2004; TNUDP II Project Evaluation Report, 2005, p. 44.
14 TNUDP II Project Evaluation Report, 2005, pp. 71–72.
15 TNUDF Activity Report, 2003–2004.
16 WSPF – Objectives, Structure, Security and Credit Enhancements 2002.
17 The longest tenure of municipal bonds issued in India was ten years.
18 Fitch Ratings (2003). Water and Sanitation Pooled Fund (WSPF) rating rationale, p. 2.
19 The long-term government security rate in that period was 9 per cent (RBI, 2002).
20 Memorandum of private placement for non-convertible redeemable bonds issued by WSPF, 2002.

References

El-Daher, S. (1997). 'Municipal Bond Markets: Experience of the USA', Infrastructure notes, Transportation, Water and Urban Development. Washington, DC: World Bank.

—— (2000). 'Specialized Financial Intermediaries for Local Governments: A Market-based Tool for Local Infrastructure Finance', Infrastructure notes, Urban sector. Washington, DC: World Bank.

Epstein, P., Peterson, G.E., Pigey, J.H., DeAngelis, M. and Sherer, S. (2000). 'Municipal Credit Market Development in Bulgaria: Policy and Legal Framework', East European Regional Housing Sector Assistance Project. Washington, DC: The Urban Institute.

FIRE (1999a). 'Urban Performance Indicators Systems: A Comparative Approach to Monitoring Urban Performance and Application in Tamil Nadu'. New Delhi: Indo-US Financial Institutions Reform and Expansion Project.

—— (1999b). 'The Ahmedabad Municipal Bond Issue: India's First Without a Guaranty', Debt Market component (FIRE-D) Project Note No. 17. New Delhi: Indo-US Financial Institutions Reform and Expansion Project.

—— (2001). 'Lessons Learned from the Ahmedabad Municipal Bond', Debt Market component (FIRE-D) Project Note No. 25. New Delhi: Indo-US Financial Institutions Reform and Expansion Project.

—— (2003). 'Pooled Finance Model for Water and Sanitation Projects: The Tamil Nadu Water and Sanitation Pooled Fund', Debt Market component (FIRE-D) Project Note No. 31. New Delhi: Indo-US Financial Institutions Reform and Expansion Project.

Freire, M., Petersen, J., Huertas, M. and Valadez, M. (eds) (2004). *Sub-National Capital Markets in Developing Countries – From Theory to Practice*. Washington, DC: World Bank and Oxford University Press.

Ghodke, M. (2004). 'Accessing Capital Markets by Urban Local Bodies in India: An

Assessment of Municipal Bonds', in *India Infrastructure Report*, 3iNetwork. New Delhi: Oxford University Press.

Guhan, S. (1986). 'State Finances in Tamil Nadu: 1960–85. A Review of Trends and Policy', Working Paper no. 77. Chennai: Madras Institute of Development Studies.

IADF (2004). 'Financing Local Government', *International Association of Development Funds Bulletin*, 1(1), March.

Johnson, B. (2004). 'Innovative Pooled Financing Mechanisms for Local Infrastructure Investments', Presentation to the Innovative Water and Wastewater Financing Workshop for the ANE Region, Manila, Philippines, 15–17 March 2004.

Joshi, R. (2004). 'Value for Money and Municipal Accounting Reforms', in *India Infrastructure Report*, 3iNetwork. New Delhi: Oxford University Press.

Kehew, R., Matsukawa, T. and Petersen, J. (2005). 'Local Financing for Sub-sovereign Infrastructure in Developing Countries: Case Studies of Innovative Domestic Credit Enhancement Entities and Techniques', Discussion Paper No. 1, Infrastructure, Economics and Finance Department. Washington, DC: World Bank.

Leigland, J. (1997). 'Accelerating municipal bond market development in emerging economies: An assessment of strategies and progress', *Public Budgeting and Finance*, 17(2): 8.

Marfitsin, V., Tokoun, L., Makagonov, P. and Ivanov, V. (1997). 'Russia: Regional and Local Borrowing', in Phelps, P. (ed.), 'Municipal Bond Market Development', USAID Finance Working Paper. Washington, DC: USAID.

Mathur, M.P. (2002). 'Alandur sewerage project: A unique experiment of public participation in project financing', in *India Infrastructure Report*, 3iNetwork. New Delhi: Oxford University Press.

Matoušková, Z., Tacjman, P. and Peterson, G.E. (1997). 'Monitoring Report Municipal Infrastructure Financing Program Czech Republic', USAID Working Paper. Washington, DC: USAID.

Mukundan, K. (2005). 'Analytical Note on TNUDP and its Impact on Municipal Capacities', South Asia Energy and Infrastructure Unit (SASEI). Washington, DC: World Bank.

Orial, L.N. (2003). 'Philippines', in Yun-Hwan, K., *Local Government Finance and Bond Markets*. Manila: Asian Development Bank.

Peterson, G.E. (1996). 'Using Municipal Development Funds to Build Municipal Credit Markets'. New Delhi: Government of India and World Bank.

—— (1998). *Measuring Local Government Credit Risk and Improving Creditworthiness*, Washington, DC: World Bank.

—— (2000), 'Building Local Credit Systems', Background series, Municipal Finance. Washington, DC: World Bank.

—— (2003). *Banks or Bonds? Building a Municipal Credit Market*. Washington, DC: Urban Institute.

Phelps, P. (ed.) (1997). 'Municipal Bond Market Development', USAID Finance Working Paper. Washington, DC: USAID.

Pradhan, H.K. (2003). 'India', in Yun-Hwan, K., *Local Government Finance and Bond Markets*. Manila: Asian Development Bank.

Sood, P. (2004). 'India', in Freire, M., Petersen, J., Huertas, M. and Valadez, M. (eds.), *Sub-National Capital Markets in Developing Countries – From Theory to Practice*. World Bank and Oxford University Press.

Subrahmanyam, S.K. and Choudhury, R.C. (2004). *Functional and Financial Devolution on Panchayats in India*. Hyderabad: National Institute of Rural Development.

Temel, J.W. (2001). *The Fundamentals of Municipal Bonds*, 5th edition. The Bond Market Association.

USAID (1997). 'USAID/Philippines Initiatives and Activities with the Private Sector'. Washington, DC: USAID.

World Bank (1999). 'Project Appraisal Document for the Second Tamil Nadu Urban Development Project'. Washington, DC: World Bank.

—— (2005). 'Implementation Completion Report for the Second Tamil Nadu Urban Development Project'. Washington, DC: World Bank.

CHAPTER SIX

Intergovernmental Fiscal Transfers

Nick Devas

Introduction: objectives of intergovernmental transfers

This chapter covers the full range of transfers from central government to sub-national and local governments, including:

- Tax/revenue sharing

- General (block) grants

- Specific (conditional) grants

- Deficit grants

- Capitalisation grants

- Subsidised loans.

Primary objectives for a transfer system

The following are the primary objectives of intergovernmental fiscal transfers:

- To ensure that sub-national governments have the resources to carry out the functions assigned to them, and so to achieve vertical balance between levels of government;

- To distribute resources equitably between sub-national governments according to their relative needs and fiscal capacities, and so to achieve horizontal balance between local governments;

- To compensate for spill-over effects, where the services of one local government (e.g. a secondary school) are used by people outside that local government area;

- To achieve the right balance between national objectives, control and local discretion, and accountability, including influencing the spending patterns of local government.

Other objectives

Transfer systems may also be designed to achieve certain other objectives:

- To control the overall levels of local government expenditure;

- To encourage the mobilisation of local revenues;

- To encourage responsibility and accountability in local decision-making;

- To stimulate local economic development;

- To provide for emergency situations (e.g. natural disasters).

There may, however, be overlaps and conflicts between these objectives.

Tax or revenue sharing

Tax or revenue sharing is the sharing with the sub-national/local government of all or part of the revenue from a particular national tax (e.g. income tax) or revenue source (e.g. royalties on the extraction of natural resources such as minerals, oil or gas). This may be:

- By origin (that is, a proportion of the revenue is shared on the basis of where it was collected) – derivation principle;

- By a formula.

Compared to grants, revenue shares tend to be more secure, since they are usually defined in law and so are not subject to annual decision by central government. They are also usually more buoyant, since they are based on a specified percentage of a national revenue source, which is more likely than local revenue sources to respond automatically to inflation, population growth and economic growth. However, high rates of tax sharing (for example, those specified in constitutions) can undermine the incentive of central government to collect the tax.

Unlike grants, for which allocations are clearly in the hands of central government, revenue sharing suggests a partnership between central and local government, in which the latter may play a significant role in mobilising the revenues – even collecting them.

Tax sharing generally involves local discretion in the use of the revenues but not in the tax rate, and hence in the amount received, unlike a local own revenue source or a system of local surcharging on a national tax (sometimes called tax-base sharing).

Sharing by origin gives local government an incentive to assist in revenue mobilisation. With sharing by formula, that incentive is greatly reduced, since any revenue effort merely increases the size of the pool from which the particular local government receives only a formula share. But inter-regional inequities, and difficulties of assigning shared revenue to the right local government, may necessitate the use of a formula basis, e.g. per capita allocations (as with the business rate in the UK), or allocation based on some other factors to reflect local expenditure needs. In such cases, revenue sharing may be little different from a grant.

General (block) grants

General grants are designed to contribute to the costs of some or all of the services provided by local government. As such, they are intended to address both vertical and horizontal imbalances. General grants allow local governments discretion over the use of money, but there may be limitations/exclusions as to what can be financed and conditions as to use. An important aspect is whether grants can be used to finance debt-servicing on past borrowing (as they can in the UK).

General grants require an allocation formula to distribute grants equitably between local governments, taking account of differences in local expenditure need and relative local fiscal capacity. Block grants are the principal mechanism for achieving equalisation of resources between local governments.

Part (or all) of a block grant can be made conditional on the achievement of particular performance objectives, such as increased local revenue, service delivery performance or financial reporting. An example is the local government transfer fund in Kenya. Such grant elements need an effective system for monitoring on performance. As with any performance target system, there are risks of data manipulation and perverse incentives.

Specific grants

Specific grants are intended to cover some (or all) of the costs of a particular service or activity or development. Grants may be calculated as a share of the agreed costs of a service or project (in the UK, the central government meets 50 per cent of the agreed costs of the police service), or as a fixed amount per unit of the service (e.g. a set sum of money per km of road maintained).

Cost-sharing specific grants may be cash-limited (i.e. a cash amount fixed in advance), or they may be open-ended (i.e. allow for adjustments to reflect increased actual costs during the year or during the life of the project).

Specific grants allow central government to determine the priorities, the nature of the service to be provided or the project to be developed, in any level of detail. However, detailed central specification may conflict with local needs and priorities, and may lead to an inefficient use of resources unless there is flexibility to adapt to local situations. Also, fungibility of money (that is, the fact that all money is the same) means that specific grants may substitute for, rather than supplement, local resources for a particular sector, and effectively allow a local government to increase spending on an area not intended by central government.

Variations of specific grants

- *Staff grants:* To meet the costs of all the staff employed by local government (e.g. the former Subsidi Daerah Otonom (SDO) in Indonesia and grants for staff costs in

Ghana), or of certain staff, e.g. teachers. Such grants are likely to encourage local governments to employ more staff and may lead them to use staff inefficiently.

- **Matching grants:** For certain types of activity or project that central governments wish to promote, a matching grant is made on condition that local government makes a matching contribution (not necessarily 50:50 – the matching contribution may be varied according to the fiscal capacity of the local government). Matching grants can be used to encourage local revenue mobilisation, as well as to direct local spending in a particular way favoured by central government. However, richer local governments, which can afford the matching contributions, will be the main beneficiaries, unless matching shares are varied according to local fiscal capacity.

- **Emergency grants:** Such grants are usually made to deal with natural disasters. But such allocations should be limited to real emergencies: if they become handouts in response to any unbudgeted need, they undermine local accountability.

Other possible transfers

Deficit grants have been used in some countries to make up the difference between a local government's actual expenditures and its revenues. Such an arrangement might appear attractive, but it tends to discourage both local revenue effort and efficient use of resources by the local government, since local governments know that central government will make up any shortfall. Such grants also tend to shift responsibility for local spending decisions to central government and to undermine local accountability. They are, therefore, a very unsatisfactory way of providing transfers.

Initial capitalisation: Sometimes used for special purpose agencies, such as a development corporation, where investment can generate revenues. This model is not appropriate for local governments in a devolved system.

Central budget allocations: In some cases, local governments may be given authority to draw specified amounts from central budget for particular purposes. This is most likely where the local government is acting as a field agent of central government in relation to a particular activity or delegated function.

Competitive bidding for grants (e.g. the UK's Challenge Funding): This can encourage initiative, quality and performance, but will reward those local governments which have the greatest capacity to respond. Thus, such a system should only be used for modest supplementary grants and not for basic funding.

Subsidised loans: Loans on less than market rates of interest involve a (disguised) subsidy. There are significant risks in this:

- It may lead to inappropriate investments if a local government is not faced with the true costs of the investment (a former subsidised loan scheme for the construction of local markets in Indonesia resulted in markets being in inappropriate locations);

- Rich local governments will be the main beneficiaries, because they can afford to borrow most;

- Such loan subsidies distort the horizontal balance between local governments in the allocation of central transfers.

Evaluating transfer systems

Intergovernmental transfer systems can be evaluated against a number of criteria: adequacy, elasticity and stability; inter-regional equity; economic efficiency and incentives; simplicity, practicality and transparency.

Adequacy, elasticity, stability

- The total level of resources transferred to local government needs matches the responsibilities assigned, in order to ensure vertical balance.

- Transfer amounts need to be adjusted each year to reflect inflation and demographic changes, to ensure that real per capita resources are maintained; where the economy is growing, transfers should also reflect that real growth.

- Revenue sharing may be more elastic than grants, since it is based on buoyant national taxes; however, if the economy declines, tax revenues, and hence revenue shares, may decline.

- Allocation formulae must avoid creating significant fluctuations in transfers from one year to another; frequent changes in allocation formulae can be very destabilising.

- Local governments need to know transfer allocations well in advance to enable them to prepare their budgets.

- Approved transfers must actually be paid, and paid on time.

Inter-regional equity

- Revenue sharing by origin will reflect and reinforce inter-regional economic differences.

- Block grants can compensate for this if allocations take account of local fiscal capacity; however, there is a major problem of how to measure local fiscal capacity objectively (since actual local revenues reflect both local fiscal capacity and local fiscal effort); also, the scale of block grant resources available is unlikely to fully offset the differences in revenue capacity between the richest and poorest local governments.

- Allocation formulae should also take account of objective differences in expenditure needs, but not of differences in expenditure levels resulting from political choices; again there are problems in measuring needs objectively.

- Formulae may also take account of cost variations due to objective factors, such as remoteness, transport costs, and geographical and physical conditions, but not cost variations which merely reflect differences in efficiency.

- Recurrent expenditure needs may differ from development expenditure needs: the former may be higher in well-developed regions, which already have a range of facilities to maintain and operate; while the latter will be higher in less developed regions with fewer facilities.

It should be noted that transfer systems are concerned with inter-jurisdictional equity, that is, the distribution of resources between local governments. This is quite different from inter-personal equity. Intergovernmental grants to poor regions may do little for poor people in those regions – that depends on how the local government uses the resources – nor for poor people in the rich regions.

Economic efficiency and incentives

- Grant systems should be designed to encourage efficient use of resources by local governments. This means that, ideally, grants should target outputs, not inputs (i.e. grants should relate to the delivery of a service, rather than be a subsidy for the staff of the local government or capital costs, which might encourage an inefficient use of staff or capital resources).

- Grants should encourage local governments to make their expenditures conform with national development objectives, but should allow the flexibility to adapt to local conditions; otherwise, resources will be wasted on projects which are not needed or which are unsuited to local conditions.

- Grants should avoid discouraging local revenue mobilisation; without an incentive element in the grant system to encourage local revenue collection, grants may simply substitute for local revenues.

- In practice, even specific grants may lead to unintended expenditures, as a result of 'shunting' or 'displacement' (e.g. the availability of grants for schools may mean that a local government can use its own resources for building offices rather than schools). This is because money is fungible.

Simplicity, practicality and transparency

- The grant system and formulae need to be sufficiently simple to be generally understood.

- The system should use only data that are available for every local government, and which are sufficiently reliable and not open to manipulation by the local government.

- Grant allocation formulae need to be transparent, and allocations should be published.

Issues for the design of intergovernmental transfers

a) *Dependence of local governments on the centre* erodes local autonomy and accountability. However, the fact that the central government has the main revenue sources means that no system of decentralisation can function without transfers. There are examples where local governments receive a large proportion of their revenues from the centre without its removing their local discretion (e.g. the Netherlands) and others where local governments are highly controlled by the centre, even without receiving significant funds from above (e.g. Kenya). What matters is not the proportion of resources that comes from local revenues, but the discretion over expenditure from overall resources, and particularly 'discretion at the margin'. (Since most local government expenditure is effectively committed, what matters is the marginal choice about spending a bit more in this or a bit less on that.)

b) *There is an inherent tension between local autonomy and central direction.* A balance has to be struck between block transfers (including revenue shares) that allow local discretion to reflect local needs, conditions and priorities, and specified or conditional transfers to finance those functions where there is a clear national priority or requirement for uniform national standards. In the early stages of decentralisation, it is generally considered desirable to retain a substantial conditional grant element, to ensure that resources are used for essential services and not diverted into low priority areas like offices and vehicles (but recognising that information asymmetries and fungibility limit the centre's ability to enforce conditions).[1] In the end, that balance has to be arrived at through the negotiation of central-local relations.

c) *Transfers may substitute for local revenues and thus erode local revenue effort.* Again, the fact that the main (and most neutral and equitable) taxes are centrally collected in most countries means that transfers are essential. Local governments still have an incentive to collect local revenues, since transfers finance only part of the costs of services demanded by local citizens. Nevertheless, rising grant allocations often do erode local revenue effort, especially where local taxes are difficult to collect (e.g. Uganda). To counteract that, grant systems can incorporate incentive factors to reward revenue performance.

d) *The intergovernmental transfer system should be designed to achieve balance:* vertical balance (between levels) and horizontal balance (between local governments at the same level). This requires a proper analysis of the expenditure needs created by the assignment of functions to each local government, and the revenue capacity of each local government (see below). Where there is more than one level of local government, resources need to be allocated fairly between levels to reflect the distribution of responsibilities.

There will always be competing demands for scarce resources from central ministries and national programmes, and these may often carry more weight than the needs of local government. In some countries (e.g. Nigeria), there are constitutional provisions for resource distribution between levels of government; while these may protect essential resources for local government, they can lead to inflexibility, and to circumvention by central government.

e) **Distribution between types of transfer:** Within the overall system of transfers, a key decision is what proportions should go via the different forms of transfer:[2]

- Tax sharing: for buoyancy, partnership, local discretion

- Specific grants: for specific national programmes or objectives

- Block grants: for local discretion and fiscal equalisation.

f) **Allocations of grants and transfers to local governments should be based on clear and technically sound formulae.** In the end, though, allocations are politically determined. At one extreme, allocations may be based on ad hoc negotiations, so that those regions which have the greatest political bargaining power receive the largest amounts. Even where there are clear allocation formulae, these may be manipulated to favour particular regions or politically favoured jurisdictions. Allocations may be further manipulated after they have been approved, through top-slicing by ministries or by intermediate levels of government, or they may be paid late, or not at all. All of those things undermine the credibility of the intergovernmental transfer system and the viability of local governments.

g) **Allocation formulae need to strike a balance between fairness and simplicity.** In order to achieve horizontal and vertical balance, it is desirable to take into account all the factors that affect local governments' abilities to finance their expenditure requirements. However, the data required for such comprehensive formulae are unlikely to be available, and much of the data that are available may be unreliable, out of date or subject to manipulation (and the formulae can only work if reliable data are available for *all* local governments). In addition, the more complex the formula, the less it is likely to be understood and the more scope there is for political manipulation. There is a good case for keeping the formulae simple and understandable, even if they does not achieve complete equity.

A study by de Mello (2000) of published data on 30 developed and developing countries sought to identify whether intergovernmental transfers resulted in a 'deficit bias' in decentralised decision-making, as a result of co-ordination failures, common-pool problems, free-riding and moral hazard, resulting in worsened national fiscal deficits. This concern comes particularly out of Latin America, where substantial tax sharing, not always matched by devolution of functions, together with wide borrowing powers by sub-national governments, has undermined the fiscal position of some central gov-

Financing Local Government

ernments. However, de Mello found that in most OECD countries, well-established and effective rules have generally prevented that problem. Nevertheless, these are significant potential pitfalls for fiscal decentralisation in developing and transitional countries if the system is not well designed.

Intergovernmental grant formulae

Allocation of block grants (and revenue shares allocated by formula) should be based on a transparent formula using objective factors. Formulae should include the following elements.

a) *Expenditure needs factors*

A local government's need for resources to meet its expenditure responsibilities will be determined by various factors. For example, for primary education, the main driving factor will be the number of pupils, but there will be other factors that influence costs, such as remoteness, relative poverty of the population and the condition of school buildings. There will also be differences between recurrent expenditure needs (based on the number of pupils in school) and capital expenditure needs (dependent on the number of school-age children not yet in school). However, accurate data on such factors may not be available.

In practice, for most local government services, population is likely to be the main driver of expenditure needs. But this may not adequately reflect the needs of sparsely populated regions or small local government units (with relatively high overhead costs for democratic decision-making and basic administration). Thus, an area factor and a lump sum element are often included in the formula. However, the lump sum element should be small, to avoid creating an incentive for fragmentation of local government units.

More complex formulae may include a variety of factors related to the costs of each of the services for which local government is responsible, e.g. length of roads and distribution of poor people. (The UK government's revenue support grant formula includes more than 100 factors.) However, accurate and up-to-date data may not exist for all local governments, and there are risks if the local government can manipulate the data to its advantage. Also, the more factors there are in the formula, the more difficult it is to establish the correct weighting for each factor.

b) *Unit cost factors*

Unit costs for the same service may vary significantly across the country, depending on remoteness or geographical factors (mountain areas, islands, etc.). It may, therefore, be appropriate to include factors to reflect these differences. However, accurate cost data may be difficult to obtain, so that once again the accuracy and equity of the formula has to be balanced against practicality. There is a risk that the application of crude cost factors may simply introduce new inequities.

c) Local fiscal capacity

The capacity of local governments to finance expenditures from their own resources will vary widely. Capital cities may be able to finance all of their expenditure needs from their own revenue sources, while remote rural local governments may be able to generate little by way of local revenues. Inter-regional equity requires that allocation formulae incorporate a factor to reflect local revenue capacity. However, this is often the most difficult aspect to include, because of the absence of objective data on revenue potential. It is not appropriate to use actual revenues since these reflect revenue effort as well as revenue potential, and so would reward local governments that have low revenue effort as well as those with low revenue potential.

Where the main local revenue source is property tax, and where the central government is responsible for property valuation (as in the UK), the property tax roll can be used as the measure of local revenue capacity. In the absence of this, it may be possible to use data on regional income per capita or gross regional domestic product (GRDP) as a proxy for local fiscal capacity. However, it is rare for such data to exist for every local government, and in any case GRDP may not accurately reflect local governments' tax base (since local taxes may impinge on some economic sectors and not others).

d) Poverty

Given the concern with poverty reduction, it is often advocated that a poverty factor should be included within the formula. There are a number of problems with this: firstly, the choice of a definition of poverty and how that definition should be applied as a factor; secondly, whether data exist on poverty for all local governments, which is unlikely; thirdly, allocating resources to local governments based on a poverty factor does not mean the money will be spent on the poor. If the aim is to fund services for the poor, then a specific grant allocated on the basis of a poverty factor may be more appropriate than incorporating a poverty factor in a block grant formula. If there is a revenue capacity factor in the formula, that should already reflect poverty to some extent.

e) Revenue incentive

If there is concern about the grant system undermining local revenue performance, then it may be appropriate to include a factor in the grant formula to reflect improvements in revenue collection. This could be based on the percentage increase in revenue collection. Again, there will be problems in obtaining accurate and timely data, which need to be verified to avoid manipulation by local governments. Improved (or worsened) revenue performance could also be due to circumstances beyond the control of the local government.

f) Performance factors

Other performance factors can be built into the formula. In Kenya, for example, 40 per cent of the local authority transfer fund grant is allocated according to performance elements, such as submission of accounts, progress on debt reduction and preparation of a service delivery plan using citizen participation. Such incentive elements can be effective in achieving improved performance (as has been the case in Kenya), although they require effective and uncorrupt mechanisms for checking on actual performance.

In summary, of the above elements, expenditure needs should probably be the dominant one. Within that, population is likely to be the dominant factor (and the one on which reliable data are most likely to exist). There will rarely be sufficient resources to achieve complete equalisation of fiscal capacity between local governments, but where inter-regional inequalities are large, a substantial proportion of the block grant should be allocated for equalisation, so long as objective data are available to reflect local revenue potential. Performance factors, including revenue mobilisation, can be added, providing there are mechanisms for monitoring actual performance. Other factors, including poverty weighting, raise problems about data availability and possible perverse incentives.

In the end, there needs to be a balance between the fairness of the grant allocation, as reflected in the above factors, and simplicity. If the formula is too complex, it becomes impractical to apply and cannot be readily understood and accepted by those who receive the grant. Complexity also opens up the opportunity for manipulation.

There will need to be central controls (e.g. through external audit) to ensure that grant money is not misused. However, controls should not necessarily be more stringent than controls over the use of local revenues: grant monies do not 'belong' to central government – all money belongs to the taxpayer, and there should therefore be proper systems of control over the use of all money used by local (and central) government.

Finally, the impact of the transfer system on local governments should be monitored regularly, so that undesirable results can be corrected. However, the system also requires stability – frequent changes to the formula are destabilising for decentralised service provision.

Notes

1 A positive example here is the LGDP grant in Uganda, which allows local governments at various levels to select local development projects from a menu. This allows quite wide scope for local choice about the type, design and location of projects, but ensures that resources are used broadly for national priority sectors.

2 In addition, there may be flows of funds from the centre to the locality through sector expenditures of sectoral ministries and special purpose agencies that by-pass local government.

References and further reading

Ahmad, E. (ed.) (1997). *Financing Decentralized Expenditures: An International Comparison of Grants*. Cheltenham: Edward Elgar.

Bird, R.M. and Tarasov, A.V. (2004). 'Closing the Gap: Fiscal Imbalances and Inter-governmental Transfers in Developed Federations', *Environment and Planning C*, 22: 77–102.

Bird, R.M. and Vaillancourt, F. (eds) (1999). *Fiscal Decentralization in Developing Countries*. Cambridge: Cambridge University Press.

de Mello, L.R. (2000). 'Fiscal Decentralization and Inter-Governmental Fiscal Relations: A Cross-Country Analysis', *World Development*, 28(2).

Devas, N. (2002). 'Issues in Fiscal Decentralisation: Ensuring Resources Reach (the Poor at) the Point of Service Delivery', Paper to the DFID Workshop on Improving Service Delivery in Developing Countries, Eynsham Hall, 24–30 November 2002. Available at http://139.184.194.47/go/display&type=Document&id=410

Shah, A. (1994). *The Reform of Intergovernmental Fiscal Relations in Developing and Emerging Market Economies*. Washington, DC: World Bank.

Smoke, P. (2001). 'Fiscal Decentralization in Developing Countries: a Review of Current Concepts and Practices', UNRISD, Democracy and Human Rights Programme Paper 2, available at http://139.184.194.47/go/display&type=Document&id=452

Ter-Minassian, T. (ed.) (1997). *Fiscal Federalism in Theory and Practice*. Geneva: International Monetary Fund.

CHAPTER SEVEN

Budgeting and Expenditure Management in Local Government

....

Nick Devas

Roles of financial planning and budgeting

There are three key roles for financial planning and budgeting in local government. Firstly, policy-making involves setting expenditure priorities in line with policies and plans, and then allocating the available resources in line with those priorities. The policy-making role also involves choices about local tax rates, together with tariffs for fees and charges, so as to generate sufficient resources to meet the planned expenditure. Secondly, financial planning can be used as a management tool, to provide financial information for the managers of services and programmes, to ensure that expenditure programmes deliver value for money, and to monitor revenue and expenditure performance during the year. Thirdly, it can be a mechanism of control, through the authorisation of expenditures, prevention of abuse and fraud, and ensuring solvency by preventing fiscal deficits.

Plans and budgets also serve as instruments for citizen participation and local government accountability, enabling citizens and civil society to engage with local decision-makers about the use of available resources, and subsequently to hold the local government to account for their actual use.

Annual budgets should reflect longer-term development plans and policies, as well as any medium-term financial and expenditure plans, such as a medium-term expenditure framework (MTEF), which should provide the framework for the annual budget. The longer the time scale, the broader the plan needs to be because of the degree of uncertainty. Thus, long- and medium-term plans need to identify broad strategies, whereas annual budgets need to be detailed for purposes of financial control.

Plans and budgets seek to identify:

- Objectives and targets for revenue and expenditure programmes

- Future expenditure needs

- Future resource availability

- Changes in circumstances which will affect needs and resources

- Constraints and opportunities

- Strategies for achieving objectives within the constraints

- Priorities between alternative uses of resources.

Recurrent and capital budgets

It is normal to distinguish between recurrent and capital budgets (the former is some-times referred to as the revenue budget). The recurrent budget covers all expenditures for ongoing activities, including wages and salaries, operating costs, maintenance costs and transfer payments (e.g. welfare payments and transfers to lower levels). It also includes debt servicing (although the repayment of the principal element of debt servicing may be treated separately in some budgeting systems).

Since the benefits of recurrent expenditure are used up during the course of the year, it should be financed from current income: taxes, charges and recurrent grants, and not from borrowing or asset sales.

Capital expenditure involves the creation or acquisition of new assets which last for more than one year ('lumpiness'), which can be financed from capital receipts (borrowing, asset sales or capital grants), as well as from recurrent income. However, the distinction is not always clear: small items which last for more than one year (e.g. books) are usually classified as recurrent.

Some countries adopt different definitions, e.g. plan and non-plan in India, routine and development in Indonesia. These distinctions may have an economic justification (consumption versus investment), but they may have distorting effects (failure to spend money on maintenance means that 'development' expenditure has to be incurred to rehabilitate the asset). It may also blur the distinction about the appropriate way to finance the expenditure.

It is critically important that capital financing (borrowing or asset sales) is not used to finance recurrent expenditure, since that is unsustainable. In some systems (e.g. in some central and eastern European countries), the absence of separate capital budgets has meant that when capital assets (e.g. local government-owned property) were sold, the receipts were used up on current expenditure. However, too great a separation between capital and recurrent budgets can create other problems. When planning the financial requirements of a service, it is necessary to consider both recurrent and capital expenditures together, since effective and efficient provision of a service requires an appropriate combination of capital and recurrent spending.

The sub-national government budget preparation process

The budget preparation process usually occupies most of the year preceding the budget. It involves a number of stages.

a) *Reviewing the context and planning framework*

This should take account of:

- National, regional and local long- and medium-term development plans, policies and priorities; the annual budget should be seen as the mechanism for implementing such plans and strategies by allocating resources to them;

- The medium-term expenditure framework, which determines the parameters for the annual budget – as such, the budget represents the first year of a three-year rolling plan and the annual budgeting process will be largely about fleshing out the details;

- A review of actual performance of revenues and expenditures during the current and previous years, against the budgets for those years;

- The opportunities for citizens to participate in identifying the needs and priorities of the locality, and whether that process takes account of different interests, for example those of poor and marginalised groups, rather than reflecting only the views of the vociferous and well connected.

b) *Revenue forecasting*

This should not be just trend extrapolation, but should be a realistic assessment of the previous year's actual revenue performance and the factors that may affect revenues in the coming year, including exogenous factors which may affect revenue (e.g. changes in the local or national economy and changes in government policy which may affect local revenues). It should also take account of the scope for increasing revenue collection performance (increased effectiveness – but this needs to be realistic, so as to avoid revenue shortfalls during the year), and for revising tax and charge rates (especially those fixed in money terms) in line with inflation, and projecting the impact on the revenues of higher tax rates.

c) *Estimating expenditure requirements*

Recurrent expenditure estimates should:

- Be based on current commitments (i.e. the continuing costs of current services);

- Adjusted for inflation (this is usually best handled centrally by the finance department on a consistent basis for the whole budget, with spending departments preparing proposals at constant prices);

- Identify potential cost savings from greater efficiency or alternative ways of delivering services;

- Incorporate new commitments (recurrent cost implications of new commitments, e.g. operations and maintenance, and the debt-servicing implications of capital developments; effects of changes in national legislation or requirements; effects of approved changes in policy);

- Add in costs of proposed improvements to service provision.

It is important that estimates prepared by departments within the local government should be based on adequate guidance in advance from the municipal finance department about resource limits and policy priorities. This enables those managing the services to plan realistically within the resources available. In the absence of such guidance, spending departments are likely to bid high ('pad their bids') in the expectations of cuts, obliging the central finance department to make arbitrary decisions about cuts in budget proposals later in the process. However, this does require an appropriate mechanism for making broad resource allocations between departments or sectors. These are strategic choices which need to be made by elected representatives through a proper policy process based on agreed objectives and strategies.

Capital expenditure requirements will include previously agreed projects and proposed additional projects. Ideally, all projects should be subject to proper project (cost benefit) appraisal as part of the planning process, and future recurrent cost implications should be identified.

d) *Balancing the budget*

Invariably, expenditure needs exceed available revenue. Difficult choices have to be made. The options are:

- Increasing revenue, by raising tax or charge rates (but forecasted revenues need to be realistic, since unrealistic forecasts can lead to unplanned budget deficits or unplanned expenditure cuts during the year);

- Cutting expenditures;

- Drawing down reserves – if they are available;

- Budgeting for a deficit – something which no system of decentralised government finance allows.

Balancing the budget is essentially a political process. Although the municipal finance department may manage the process, ultimately decisions need to be taken by elected representatives, since these are strategic choices. The process needs to be as open and transparent as possible, and it must be guided by agreed policies and strategies of the elected council.

e) *Formal approval of the budget*

Approval must be given before the beginning of the financial year if budgetary control is to be effective. As well as approval by the elected council of the local government, the central (or state/provincial) government may have to give its approval. Delays in approval undermine the budget as a tool of expenditure management.

Some issues in local government budgeting

Input versus output budgets

Most conventional budgets are prepared in input terms: line items for wages/salaries, materials, transport, etc. Such budgets are useful for controlling expenditure, but give no indication of output, and nothing against which performance can be judged.

Ideally, budgets should be based around expenditure programmes with clear objectives, service standards, outputs and performance targets. Programme outputs can then be linked to the input costs in line-item terms needed to achieve the outputs. However, outputs and performance targets may be difficult both to specify and to measure. PPBS (programme performance budgeting system) is the classic form of programme budgeting, but is generally regarded as too complex and elaborate. Nevertheless, some attempt to specify outputs and performance targets, and to relate inputs to outputs, is essential if resources are to be better used. Without an indication of outputs, the only measure of performance is whether the money is spent, rather than what has been achieved.

Incremental budgeting

Most conventional budgets are incremental: planned expenditures are based on the previous year's expenditures plus an allowance for inflation or service improvements. Such budgeting is easy to do and offers relatively stability. However, it never challenges whether the activity is really necessary, or whether it could be carried out in other more efficient ways.

Bean and Hussey (1998) have summarised the advantages and disadvantages of incremental budgeting:

Advantages	Disadvantages
• Simple	• Historic
• Quick	• No account taken of necessary future changes
• Accurate if little change in activity	• Assumes the base is accurate
	• Compounds historic errors

Zero-based budgeting

Zero-based budgeting (ZBB) is one alternative to incremental budgeting, but is generally regarded as over-elaborate and unrealistic in most situations. However, selective use of ZBB can be valuable, for example, taking a particular service where there may be large inefficiencies and specifying from scratch what is required to achieve the output objectives and the costs of achieving these outputs. Contract specification for contracted-out (or out-sourced) services is a comparable process to ZBB, since it requires outputs and performance to be clearly specified in advance.

Some of the advantages and disadvantages of ZBB are shown in the box below (Bean and Hussey, 1998).

Advantages	Disadvantages
• Proactive • Realistic and accurate • Links into business plans	• Time-consuming • Requires clear objectives • Many organisations do not have a zero base, as they have to work with the staff, buildings and resources they inherit from year to year

Realistic revenue forecasts

The tendency of municipal governments in some countries is to inflate revenue forecasts to fit the projected level of expenditure, thereby pretending to show a balanced budget. This can be highly damaging, since actual revenue collection will fall well short of the forecast, with the result that the local government will run out of money during the year and arbitrary cuts will have to be made. This undermines the legitimacy and accountability of the budget process, and puts power into the hands of a few people (e.g. the mayor or the finance director) to make arbitrary allocation decisions during the year (Devas, 2003).

Unintended commitments

It is important to avoid unintended commitments. These can arise where approval is given to make a start on a major capital project without taking adequate account of the capital and recurrent cost implications in future years. Once the full costs become apparent, it may be politically difficult to abandon the project. This strategy is often used by project managers to establish incremental commitments to projects.

Consolidated budgets

Proper choices about resource use and transparency of decision-making require that all resources are treated together in one budget. While there may be separate accounts for specific services, these should all be brought together in one consolidated budget. The non-transparent nature of 'extra-budgetary' accounts and special funds provides scope for corruption and clientelistic decision-making.

Participatory budgeting

In Brazil, municipal governments have experimented with participatory budgeting (PB). Under PB, local communities are able to consider expenditure priorities affecting their neighbourhood (Souza, 2001). These are fed through into the municipal budget. Although the range of choice is often quite limited (city governments still exert tight control over the process), it has resulted in some redirection of expenditure towards the poor, wider participation of previously excluded groups and greater transparency over budgetary decisions.

The model has been emulated by local governments in a number of countries. There are also other ways in which greater participation in budgetary choices can occur:

- Giving local elected councillors a small budget for local priorities identified through a participatory process (although this tends to reinforce the clientelistic relationship of councillors with their electorate, as well as potentially giving an unfair electoral advantage to the incumbent);

- Giving 'area committees' of the elected council some spending powers in relation to their area;

- Establishing lower levels of elected local governance below the municipality, each with their own resources and budgets (Devas, 2003).

Expenditure management

a) *Financial procedures*

Expenditure management procedures need to define rules about authorising orders and payments, checking bills and recording payments. They must also include a method for approving virements, also known as re-appropriations (that is, the ability to move resources between budget heads).

Virements allow a degree of flexibility to deal with unforeseen or changed circumstances. A balance is required between the need for flexibility and the need for control – if there is too much flexibility, the budget does not serve the purpose of determining what happens.

b) *Revised or supplementary budgets*

Unforeseen or changed circumstances can also be handled by revised or supplementary budgets during the course of the year, but these undermine the credibility of the original budget. Frequent revisions make nonsense of the budgeting process, and revised budgets may be subject to less rigorous scrutiny than the original budget, raising issues about political choices and transparency. There is also the problem of where additional resources come from, if they are needed. If budgets are revised so that they can allocate surplus revenue, it might be better to retain the surpluses and allocate them through the proper budgeting process in the following year.

c) *Financial information system to monitor budget implementation*

There is a need for an effective financial information system to provide programme managers with timely financial information and to provide finance staff with information on the progress of the budget, including providing early warning of problems such as over- or under-expenditure or of shortfalls in revenue. Such information needs to be provided in a timely manner and in a format which makes identification of problems easy. Computerisation can help, providing systems are properly designed.

d) *Final accounts, auditing and accountability*

Final accounts need to be produced on time, say within six months of the end of the financial year, and submitted to the elected council. They should be audited by an independent external auditor (usually appointed by central government), and the auditor's report should be submitted to the elected council. In addition, there should be systems of internal audit, concerned with ensuring that systems are secure and prevent fraud. Both internal and external audit should be concerned not just with probity but also with effectiveness (achieving objectives or targets), efficiency (costs of services) and value for money. Information on budgets, accounts and audit reports should be made available to the public in ways that can be easily understood, as a means of holding the local government to account. (See chapter 8 for more detail on accounting and auditing.)

e) *Decentralised financial management to cost or budget centres*

These days, it is common for at least some financial management responsibilities to be decentralised to service managers within the local government – whether departmental heads or lower level managers who are responsible for particular services. The units to which financial management responsibility is decentralised are usually called cost centres or budget centres (or profit centres if they are net revenue generators). In the UK, a prime example is the decentralisation of financial management to school governors. Heads of local government contractor units also have to have a high degree of decentralised financial responsibility if they are to compete with private sector contractors in competitive tenders.

Decentralised financial management requires the manager to deliver specified service levels and performance within an approved budget. It has the advantages of encouraging service managers to:

• Plan so as to make the best use of available resources, rather than 'padding' their budget submissions for others (e.g. the central finance office) to cut;

• Use available resources most efficiently – efficiency improvements are rewarded by being allowed to retain some or all of the savings within the budget centre to use to improve the service or reward staff, rather than being penalised by having to return any efficiency savings to the Treasury at year end;

- Collect all the revenue due for the service, since increased revenue means more resources available for the service.

However, decentralised financial management requires a proper system for deciding on the initial allocation of resources to each service, and proper specification of output or service levels and performance targets. There must also be systems of monitoring performance against targets, so as to hold service managers accountable, and financial controls to prevent misuse of resources. Service managers need skills in financial management, although they can be assisted by specialist finance people. The success of decentralised management also depends on an 'internal market', so that cost centres can trade with each other, e.g. buy services from one another (and perhaps from an external agency).

f) *Cash-limited financial management*

Where financial pressures are severe, and/or revenues are difficult to forecast, a system of cash-limited budgeting may be introduced. Under such a system, the finance department releases only the money that is received in the previous month, even if it is less than what is in the budget. This ensures that a deficit is not incurred.

While, under certain circumstances, cash-limited budgeting may be necessary, it tends to negate the purposes of the budget process as a means of managing expenditures in a stable and consistent manner, and can prevent the achievement of other strategic objectives. A better approach is to base budgets on more conservative and realistic revenue forecasts, and then adhere to those budgets. If actual revenues prove to be better than forecast, the surpluses can be added to reserves for use in subsequent years. However, such prudence is often difficult to achieve when both local politicians and officials demand greatly increased expenditure.

Financial management and the control of corruption

Decentralisation potentially puts more public resources at risk, in the sense that more resources are handled at locations remote from direct central controls, with more people having an influence on how the resources are used. Therefore, decentralisation may disperse corruption more widely, although it may not increase the overall level of corruption – indeed, it may help to curb it through greater accountability. Empirical evidence on the relationship between decentralisation and corruption is very mixed: for a review of the evidence from the various studies (Fjeldstad, 2004).

Nevertheless, achievement of the Millennium Development Goals requires services to be delivered throughout the country, and this requires finances to be managed in a decentralised manner, whether through local agencies of the central state or through devolved local governments. Therefore, whatever the particular mechanisms of service delivery at the local level, attention needs to be paid to financial management systems at the local level, and the capacity of both local citizens and central government to monitor resource use locally. This will involve developing secure revenue collection arrangements to prevent loss, collusion and fraud; record-keeping and accounting systems that inhibit fraud and provide automatic cross-checks; and public access to information about resource availability and use, to promote greater accountability to citizens. It will also require effective and transparent procurement and tendering arrangements, and effective auditing systems, including the development of national level, external audit capability, and systems that ensure that local governments act upon the results of external audits.

Given limited financial management capacity at the local level, this is quite a tall order, and there is no doubt that the lack of financial management capacity at the local level is one of the main obstacles to effective decentralisation. Central support in terms of skills training, development of appropriate financial management systems and central monitoring systems are all needed. However, this is also constrained by the limited capacity at the centre in many countries: capacity to know what is going on at the local level, and to take action to rectify failure. Rent-seeking behaviour by central officials and political disputes further weaken the ability of the centre to oversee local government finances. However, it is important to stress again that these are problems inherent in any system that seeks to deliver services, and therefore finance, across the country: they are not unique to decentralised (devolved) systems of government.

Reforms in financial management

Specific reforms to financial management that have been adopted in various places in recent years include:

a) Simplifying accounting systems and making them more transparent; this may include the use of accruals accounting for expenditure, to ensure that expenditure obligations incurred appear in the accounts, even if bills have not been paid;[1]

b) Computerisation of revenue collection and accounting systems, with appropriate safeguards, to facilitate cross-checking and reduce opportunities for individual discretion and manipulation;

c) Paying grants directly from the Ministry of Finance to the bank account of the subnational government or institution for which it is intended, to prevent money being sliced at intermediate stages;

d) Simplifying grant systems to increase transparency and public understanding, and publicising information about formulae and allocations, including requiring public display of information about resources for particular facilities, services or projects, as in Uganda;

e) Avoiding multiple funding sources for the same activity, which can be used to disguise how the funds are used;

f) Requiring the submission of photographic records of project implementation;

g) Selective use of independent expenditure tracking studies to trace the use of funds (Ablo and Reinikka, 1998; Dehn *et al.*, 2002);

h) Clear rules about public procurement, specification of codes of conduct for local officials and elected representatives, and arrangements for asset declarations by elected representatives and senior officials;

i) Systems of monitoring local government performance that feed into the grant system, as used in Kenya and Uganda;

j) Building local accountability through citizen report cards (India), citizen charters, participatory budgeting (Brazil) and access to information.

All this requires a change of culture and practice within central government. Decentralisation involves a shift from a direct role in service delivery to one of enabling and monitoring the work of local governments and other agencies at the local level. This requires the building up of capacity to monitor and verify effectively, and systems that minimise the scope for monitoring to be undermined by rent-seeking behaviour. It also requires central government to play its role within the system properly: dealing promptly with requirements for approval, paying agreed grants and revenue shares on time, and seeking to reinforce good practice at the local level.

Note

1   Under a cash accounting system, it is possible for unpaid debts to accumulate without these being apparent from the accounts. This has resulted in huge problems of inter-agency arrears in many countries, including Kenya, and has disguised the fact that many local authorities are effectively insolvent. On the other hand, use of accruals accounting on the revenue side can present a dangerously misleading picture where revenue collection performance is poor, since unless the debtors position is examined, what the accounts show is the revenue due rather than what has actually been received.

References and further reading

Ablo, E. and Reinikka, R. (1998). Do Budgets Really Matter: Evidence from Public Spending on Education and Health in Uganda (World Bank) (available on World Bank website)

Bean, J. and Hussey, L. (1998). *Managing the Devolved Budget*. London: HP Publications.

Blore, I., Devas, N. and Slater, R. (2004). *Municipalities and Finance: A Sourcebook for Capacity Building*. London: Earthscan. Chapters 6, 7 and 8 provide examples of improved budgeting and financial management.

Dehn J., Reinikka, R. and Svensson J, (2002). *Survey Tools for Assessing Service Delivery*. Washington, DC: World Bank.

Devas, N. (2003). 'Can City Governments in the South Deliver for the Poor: A Municipal Finance Perspective', *International Development Planning Review*, 25 (1): pp. 1–29.

Fjeldstad O.-H. (2004). *Decentralisation and Corruption: A Review of the Literature*. Bergen, Norway: Chr. Michelson Institute.

Premchand, A. (2005). *Controlling Government Spending: The Ethos, Ethics and Economic of Expenditure Management*. New Delhi: Oxford University Press.

Souza, C. (2001). 'Participatory Budgeting in Brazilian Cities: Limits and Possibilities in Building Democratic Institutions', *Environment and Urbanization*, 13(1): 159–84.

CHAPTER EIGHT

Accounting and Auditing for Local Government

Simon Delay

Accounting systems

Effective accounting systems are essential for local government, both to provide managers with the financial information they need to manage their services and to account to citizens and taxpayers for the use of public resources. There are two principal forms of accounting:

- Management accounting provides financial information to the executive (including service managers) before, during and after the financial year;

- Financial accounting provides information for those outside the executive (elected representatives, citizens and taxpayers), usually after the end of the financial year, and so is essential for public accountability.

Auditing is the mechanism which provides assurance to the public about the veracity of the accounts, and hence is essential for public accountability.

Conventional accounting is effective at identifying costs, but poor at identifying performance. Therefore, accounting as a tool needs to be combined with other approaches in order to assess the performance of a public body such as a local government.

Costs

Cost information is important in order to:

- Know the cost at which best value is obtained

- Determine the allocation of resources

- Set charges for services provided by the local government

- Monitor in-year spending

- Manage cash flow

- Review value for money as part of performance review or value-for-money audit

- Decide whether to continue to operate a particular service.

Different requirements and decisions need information about different types of cost. A number of types of cost are important:

- **Cash costs** (both direct costs and indirect costs) are generally relevant since the cash involved must be raised eventually;

- **Overhead costs:** These are the indirect part of cash costs and so are generally relevant, but there may be problems about allocating overhead costs (see below);

- **Opportunity costs:** Non-cash costs that represent income forgone by doing something (for example, the income that could have been earned in bank interest if the capital had not been invested in a particular project) – they too are relevant in many circumstances;

- **Unavoidable costs:** Those costs that would remain whatever decision is made; these should generally be ignored, but they may vary over time.

Overhead costs should be allocated between services or service units in order to establish the true costs of a service. If this is not done properly, charges for services will not reflect the true value of the resources used, and the good performance of one unit may be achieved on the back of another unit's costs. Overhead costs should be allocated in accordance with the factors that drive the underlying need for the costs to be incurred. Thus, the costs of a central building's maintenance unit might be allocated between service units according to the space occupied. As with all such allocations there is a degree of choice over the level of sophistication used. Space occupied might be adjusted for the type and condition of buildings, but this is only worth doing where there is good information about type and condition and where there is a clear understanding of how this relates to cost.

There are a number of problems with allocating overhead costs. Firstly, the calculation of the costs and the allocation formulae may be hard for service managers (and others) to understand. Secondly, there are some costs that it may not be possible to allocate to service units (for example, the costs of operating the decision-making processes of the council). Thirdly, allocating overheads to service units may blur the accountability for controlling support costs, for example where a support unit such as building maintenance can simply charge out its costs to other units in the local government without any accountability for efficiency. On the latter point, overhead allocation needs to be seen principally as a tool for managing performance; accountability for costs should rest primarily with those who are responsible for incurring the cost – in the case of buildings maintenance this would be the managers of the building maintenance operation.

Monitoring budgets

The monitoring of budgets is essential to effective financial management, not only to avoid overspending (which raises the question of where the additional cash will come from), but also to avoid underspending that might threaten performance in service delivery. However, budget monitoring provides only a limited insight into overall performance.

Budget monitoring requires a profiled budget, that is, a budget that is spread over 12 months (or possibly four quarters) to reflect expected spending patterns:

- Flat for some costs, e.g. office space;

- Seasonal for some costs, e.g. heating or air-conditioning;

- With a stepped increase where prices rise at a specific time of the year, e.g. wages;

- Specific – to reflect policy issues or specific constraints.

Budget responsibilities need to be clear: each budget should be the responsibility of one named budget officer. However, there also needs to be overall oversight to ensure that appropriate action is being taken and the overall position is understood. This is likely to be the primary responsibility of the finance department reporting to the equivalent of the chief executive.

In large councils, the volume of budget monitoring data can overwhelm the capacity to manage. In such cases, it is sensible to manage by exception – this means that the main focus of effort in the monitoring process is on those budget lines where there is a significant variation.

When variations emerge, there are a number of options for action where the variance is an overspend:

- Reduce future expenditure on the particular item;

- Transfer budgetary resources from another budget head which is (or can be) under-spent (virement);

- Use a contingency fund or reserves;

- Raise extra income;

- Borrow (or borrow more);

- (Depending on local circumstances) seek additional help from central government – in some countries central governments do provide additional support, for example where extra spending is caused by catastrophic weather conditions.

A key issue will be whether the problem can be resolved within the sub-unit which holds the budget or whether (and under what circumstances) it is a corporate problem for the local government as a whole.

Auditing: regulation of government in the UK

The British tradition involves:

- A strong framework of internal control: rules, roles, methods, level of discretion and reporting;

- A strong post-event system of auditing, including both financial audit and performance audit;

- No pre-audit or similar pre-event authorisation;

- Separate inspection functions for certain services (increasingly the norm);

- Usually an ombudsman function (a relatively recent tradition).

Principles of public audit

The UK's Public Audit Forum (www.public-audit-forum.gov.uk) identifies three key principles of public audit:

- Independence of public sector auditors from the organisation being audited;

- Wide scope of public audit, covering financial statements, regularity (or legality), propriety (or probity) and value for money;

- The ability of public auditors to make the results of their audits available to the public and to democratically elected representatives.

Some observers would argue that the final point is too limited – that the public should have the right to access all audit reports except in very limited circumstances such as genuine cases of national security

In England, there are two principal external audit bodies. The National Audit Office (NAO) (www.nao.gov.uk) is responsible for auditing central government (ministries and most non-departmental bodies operating at the national level). It is headed by the Comptroller and Auditor General, who is an officer of Parliament, not a civil servant. The NAO is controlled and financed directly by Parliament and reports to the Public Accounts Committee. It conducts most audits directly, but contracts out around 15 per cent of its work to private firms.

The Audit Commission (AC) (www.audit-commission.gov.uk) audits local government and health authorities and trusts. It is headed by part-time commissioners and a full-time chief executive, all of whom are appointed by ministers. It is nominally independent of both the executive and legislature, but provides its reports to the relevant central government ministry. The AC supervises audits conducted by others: 70 per cent by the district audit service, which it controls, and 30 per cent by private firms. It is financed mainly by audit fees. It also produces national studies and comparative performance indicators. From April 2002, it took on part of the inspection role over local government, formerly carried out by central ministries.

Some public bodies, such as state-owned industries, some non-departmental public bodies and some local delivery organisations (e.g. colleges of higher education) are audited by private firms, which usually report to a central ministry or agency.

Audit and management roles

Table 8.1 shows the respective roles of management, internal audit and external audit within the UK system.

Table 8.1. Roles of management, internal audit and external audit

	Management	Internal audit	External audit
Policy and financial control	Prime responsibility	Safeguard	Reassure
Accuracy of accounts	Prime responsibility	Normally no direct role	Check and certify
Value for money	Prime responsibility	May carry out studies	Required to carry out studies
Able to prohibit expenditure?	n/a	No	Previously in local government and police, but this is no longer so; not in central government
Recover wrongful expenditure?	n/a	No	Previously in local government and police, but no longer. Not in central government

Historically, local government auditors had the power to 'surcharge' officers and politicians who were responsible for illegal spending or for 'causing a loss' to their local government. These powers were abolished and now local governments themselves must take action under common law to recover money where officers or politicians have acted improperly.

Traditional auditing

Traditional auditing focuses on probity and accuracy of accounts. It uses a regularity approach that examines whether transactions are within the law, within budget and have been carried out according to regulations, codes of practice, etc. It also checks whether funds were applied for the purposes for which they were provided.

The problem with regularity auditing is that it only looks backwards, discovering problems that have already happened, but not problems that could happen in the future. Regularity auditing is time-consuming, and it does not ask whether transactions were wise or effective (e.g. in terms of performance).

The following two approaches seek to address the weaknesses of traditional regularity auditing.

Systems-based auditing

Systems-based auditing examines the system of internal control to see whether controls are adequate and, if they are not, reports this to the relevant authority. It then checks whether the practice complies with the claimed system of internal control by examining any deviations. This is done on a sample basis, with the sample determined by risk factors. This means that audit capacity is used more effectively and there is more chance of preventing control breaches before they are abused. However system-based auditing requires more capable auditors than traditional auditing.

Performance auditing

Auditing needs to be concerned not just with probity, but also with performance in the use of public funds: whether resources were used effectively to achieve agreed objectives and efficiently (making the best use of resources).

The UK's Audit Commission has identified three key performance criteria, commonly known as the 'three Es', for its analyses:

- *Economy:* minimising the costs of inputs (for a given output)

- *Effectiveness:* maximising outcomes (for a given input)

- *Efficiency:* the appropriate mix of inputs and outputs (or outcomes).

In the UK, auditors play a number of roles in relation to performance audit:

- Conducting national studies on best practice

- Publishing papers on management performance

- Collating national data on best value performance indicators

- Verifying performance indicators at the local level

- Auditing the best value performance plans of local governments

- Checking the adequacy of local governments' management arrangements for delivery of economy, efficiency and effectiveness, and checking whether best practice recommendations are being followed.

A best practice approach

The best practice approach makes use of league tables and other information to identify a set of relevant and interesting cases. It then looks behind the numbers in respect of the selected cases to determine what explains the results: is it a better process or is it a different policy? From that, best practice recommendations are developed. This generally works best where it is done on a comparative basis. Developing best practice recommendations requires skills that go beyond traditional auditing; it takes expert analysis and often specialist understanding of the field that it is the object of the audit.

Audit and inspection

Audit and inspection offer complementary roles in improving service delivery by local government. Traditionally in the UK, inspectors of government services were concerned with professional standards (e.g. in prisons and schools). Auditors were concerned with costs and with financial regularity and probity. Increasingly, both are concerned with issues of performance and appropriate management structures. Thus there is a possibility of overlap. Some observers criticise this, pointing to duplication of effort and the burdens imposed on those who are being audited. Others argue that this creates healthy competition between the different scrutineers to be more effective, and allows for greater innovation in conducting and reporting on oversight. In local government in England, the potential for undesirable overlap is limited by the fact that the Audit Commission is also responsible for inspecting most services: important exceptions are schools and social services.

Some issues and caveats

In all this there are dangers of over-regulation. This is perhaps a natural consequence of increased devolution and local autonomy, and the lack of trust (much of which may be justified) on the part of central government towards local government. However, audit and inspection have heavy compliance costs (as well as direct costs), putting a strain on limited capacity and possibly encouraging rent-seeking behaviour by inspectors and auditors. Over-regulation and excessive inspection and audit can discourage local initiative and risk-taking.

Competition between audit and inspection agencies may be healthy, but it may also lead to turf wars. Scrutiny efforts need to be co-ordinated to ensure greatest benefit. Moreover, there are important issues about who scrutinises the scrutineers, and who guards the guardians.

Finally, the following are some caveats about adopting innovative financial management, accounting and performance approaches, adapted from Schick (1998: 31).

Before you ...	You should ...
Introduce performance or outcome budgeting	Foster an environment that supports and demands performance
Seek to control outputs	Control inputs
Account for accruals	Account for cash
Introduce internal controls	Establish external control
Install an integrated financial management system	Operate a reliable accounting system
Budget for results to be achieved	Budget for work to be done
Introduce performance contracts in the public sector	Enforce formal contracts in the private sector
Move to performance auditing	Have effective financial auditing
Insist managers efficiently use resources entrusted to them	Adopt and implement predictable budgets

Reference

Schick, A. (1998). *Contemporary Approach to Public Expenditure Management.* Washington, DC: World Bank Institute.

CHAPTER NINE

Building Citizen Participation and Local Government Accountability

Nick Devas

Limitations of local government

The traditional view of local government is that local electors elect councillors who make decisions about local services and levy local taxes to pay for those services. The only role for citizens is to vote in elections every four years or so and pay their local taxes. This view of local governmental is being increasingly challenged. Citizens expect to have a greater say in the running of services that affect them. They are dissatisfied by the lack of accountability of those they have elected for the taxes they have levied and other resources they have used. And in many countries they are concerned about the level of corruption in local government.

Elections are, of course, a key mechanism of accountability for local government. But elections are a very crude instrument of choice. Manifestos, if they offer anything at all clearly, offer a package of generalised policies. Elections are often fought on the basis of personalities or ethnic identities. Electoral practices are often not inclusive (first-past-the-post elections tend to marginalise women and minority groups as well as the poor) and are open to abuse. Once elected, councillors may make decisions behind closed doors, without any opportunities for participation by others or accountability to citizens until the next election. Local level political processes are often dominated by local elites, who may be able to rely on patronage networks to ensure their re-election. And there is little information available on which to judge the performance of those who have been elected.

Thus, the range of choice is highly constrained, occurs only infrequently (typically, once every four years) and with little information available. Consequently, for decisions on more specific issues, other mechanisms of participation are needed. There is also the need for the development of programmatic political parties, with clear policies and manifestos, as well as for more inclusive political processes at local level.

Participatory mechanisms

Because of the limitations of representative democracy, more direct participation of citizens is needed. This is particularly the case when dealing with detailed issues – proposals for particular developments or the management of schools – which cannot be handled through the broad manifestos of political parties at infrequent elections. There are numerous participatory mechanisms:[1]

- Public meetings

- Consultation exercises

- Opinion surveys

- Referenda

- Formal grievance procedures

- Ombudsman and appeals procedures

- Participatory budgeting (PB) (see below).

One particular example is participatory budgeting. PB has been adopted by a number of municipalities in Brazil as a way of opening up the municipal budgeting process to a much larger number of people. In some cities, the process is elaborate and seeks to obtain the views of a wide cross-section of citizens, particularly the poor. PB has increased the transparency of decision-making, reduced patron-clientelism and redirected expenditure towards services for the poor. However, PB raises many issues, not least what is the relationship between this process and the elected councillors' responsibility for budget approval. (For a further discussion of participatory budgeting, see Souza (2001).)

There are often mixed motives for adopting such participatory approaches, ranging from a genuine desire to listen to the views of citizens to more cynical attempts, for example by local councillors, to manipulate and forestall opposition. Where legislation requires participation, this may be undertaken simply as a formality. At the same time, participatory processes can easily be hijacked by the articulate and powerful, so that the results do not reflect the views of the participants. Participatory processes may also disadvantage the poor, who lack the time, resources and education to participate effectively.

What matters is:

a) The attitude and commitment of the politicians (and officials) involved in the process;

b) The steps taken to ensure that the results reflect the views of all citizens (or all those affected), particularly the poor and the marginalised, and not just the articulate and powerful;

c) The resources available to implement the agreement – since there is little point in going through a participatory process if there are no resources to implement what is agreed upon.

Of course, it is important to be realistic about what can be achieved within a particular situation. The obstacles to effective participation caused by the existing power structures and power relationships at the local level need to be recognised and understood. Nevertheless, changes can and do happen over time, not least through the power of civil society.

Mechanisms of accountability

Democratic local governance requires accountability in a number of directions:

- Horizontally – of the executive to the elected representatives

- Downwards – of the elected representatives to the citizens

- Upwards – of local governments to central government, particularly for the use of funds.

Periodic elections are not sufficient, especially where information is lacking. Using the principal-agent analysis, the principals (citizens) must be able to hold their agents (the elected representatives) to account for what has been done, and the elected representatives (principals) have to hold the executive/paid officials (agents) to account. All this requires information and transparency, since the typical problem in the principal-agent relationship is asymmetry in access to information.

The following will be important in achieving local accountability:

- Mechanisms for reporting by the executive to the elected legislature;

- Publication of information about local government performance to citizens, in an understandable form;

- Preparation, approval and publication of budgets, showing the proposed use of resources;

- Preparation, approval and publication of accounts in a timely manner, showing the actual use of money;

- Auditing of accounts and publication of auditors' reports.

Publication of other performance indicators can be useful: performance against standards and targets, league tables and citizens' charters. These can do much to heighten awareness among citizens and so build local accountability. In the UK, much work has been done on this, including the publication of league tables of performance against targets, best value studies and public service agreements.

Publication by central government of grant allocations to local government and to units such as schools or health centres (as in Uganda) can also help citizens and service users to demand accountability from local government or service managers. In some systems, central government inspectors are charged with examining local government practices. Where these operate professionally, according to clear criteria and performance standards, offering constructive advice, they can do much to enhance accountability and performance. Where they act arbitrarily, or in a rent-seeking manner, their actions can be destructive.

The role of civil society

Democratic governance depends on the active participation of civil society, which includes:

- CBOs (community based organisations) or GROs (grassroots organisations);

- NGOs (national, local and international);

- Private businesses and business organisations (e.g. chambers of commerce);

- Trade unions (although these often represent only those in formal employment) and trade associations of the informal sector;

- Religious organisations;

- Traditional leaders (chiefs, elders, etc.);

- The media – local and national press and other media, as well as local radio, which is important in some countries.

Local democracy needs to be open to and responsive to civil society, and civil society can be a way of holding local government to account. Examples include (Devas *et al.*, 2004):

- Villages in some parts of India calling officials to account for the use of grant money;

- The Self-Employed Women's Association (SEWA) in India, lobbying on behalf of poor women;

- A federation of NGOs in Cebu, Philippines, scrutinising and reporting publicly on the electoral platform of mayoral candidates in terms of whether the candidates were likely to deliver on a pro-poor agenda.

Civil society is, of course, riddled with divisions – racial, ethnic, religious, political, class, income – and with conflicts of interest. It is not surprising to find that the rich and powerful tend to dominate civil society organisations. In Johannesburg, for example, the most powerful CBO is the Sandton Ratepayers Association, established to protect well-off citizens from local tax increases (Devas *et al.*, 2004). The media are often owned by business interests that have their own agenda. Even within small communities there may be major conflicts of view or interest. Thus, while being open and responsive, local governments must not listen only to the loudest voice.

Note

1   See Goetz and Gaventa (2001) for a review of a fuller range of participatory mechanisms in local governance around the world.

References

Devas, N. with Amis, P., Beall, J., Grant, U., Mitlin, D., Nunan, F. and Rakodi, C. (2004). *Urban Governance, Voice and Poverty in the Developing World.* London: Earthscan.

Goetz, A.-M. and Gaventa, J. (2001). 'Bringing Citizen Voice and Client Focus into Service Delivery', IDS Working Paper 138. Brighton: Institute of Development Studies at the University of Sussex.

Souza, C. (2001). 'Participatory budgeting in Brazilian Cities: Limits and Possibilities in Building Democratic Institutions', Urban Governance, Partnerships and Poverty Research Working Paper 28. Birmingham: IDD, University of Birmingham.

CHAPTER TEN

Local Government and Local Government Finance in England

Nick Devas

The evolution of the local government system in England[1]

Local government in England has a long history. Its origins go back to the royal charters given to some boroughs in the middle ages and to the role of the church in caring for the poor within their parishes. Elected local government developed during the early part of the nineteenth century, mainly in response to rapid urbanisation and the need to provide public services for the growing urban population.

The basic structure of English local government derives from the Local Government Act of 1972. This established a two tier system, made up of an upper tier of counties and a lower tier of districts. (There were slight variations between the metropolitan areas and the rest of the country.) These tiers are not hierarchically related: each has separate functions and each relates directly to central government, i.e. the county has no power over the district.

The 1972 Act has been amended many times, most notably to abolish the Greater London Council and the six metropolitan county councils during the 1980s, leaving single tier authorities in these areas. In addition, in some other areas (and in the whole of Scotland and Wales) the two tier system was replaced by a single tier. It was the Thatcher government's intention to replace the entire two tier system with a single tier, but opposition led to this policy being dropped after only a few single tier authorities had been created.

In the late 1990s, an upper tier of government, the Greater London Authority (GLA), was re-established for London, although the main local government functions remained with the London boroughs.

Regional government

Unlike most of continental Europe, England does not have a regional tier of government. An attempt in 2005 to establish a regional tier comparable to the elected assemblies created in Scotland and Wales was abandoned following an adverse response in the referendum about the establishment of the first of these assemblies in the north-east of England. There are, however, regional chambers, comprising representatives of central and local government, to discuss policy affecting the regions, but these have no statutory powers. There are also regional offices of central government ministries, as well as centrally appointed regional development agencies, to promote development within the regions (which have boards that include representatives of local governments). But there has never been any system of deconcentrated administration, in the sense of centrally appointed provincial governors or district administrators.

The current structure of English local government

The current structure of local government in England is a mixture of single tier and two tier authorities:

- Single tier in the six metropolitan areas, comprising 36 metropolitan district councils;

- Single tier in the 48 unitary authorities;

- Two tier in London, with the Greater London Authority plus 33 London boroughs;

- Two tier in the 34 (shire) counties plus 238 (shire) districts, with typically 5–10 districts in a county.

The current structure is shown in Table 10.1, together with the typical sizes of units. The largest single tier local authority in England (and in Europe) is the City of Birmingham (technically a metropolitan district) with a population of 1 million. Overall, the size of local governments in England is very large when compared with those of continental Europe. For example, while the UK has approximately 460 local governments for 60 million people, France has around 30,000 communes for a similar population.

Table 10.1. Local government structure in England

	Upper tier	Typical size	Lower tier	Typical size
London	Greater London Authority	9 million	33 London boroughs	150,000–300,000
6 metropolitan counties			36 metropolitan districts	100,000–1 million
34 shires	34 (shire) counties	0.5–1.5 million	238 (shire) districts	60,000–120,000
46 unitary authorities		200,000–1 million		

In addition, there is an optional lower level called the parish. Parishes do not have any mandatory functions, but local communities can choose to have one. They exist mainly in towns and rural areas. Parish councils typically cover a population of 5,000 to 25,000. There main role is consultative, although they may undertake certain limited functions such as the provision of local amenities (e.g. museums, car parking, public toilets and recreation facilities).

Table 10.2 shows the functions of English local governments, and their division between the two tiers. Unitary authorities have both sets of responsibilities. However, in London, the GLA has powers only in relation to strategic planning and transportation, with the remaining functions being carried out by the 33 London boroughs.

Table 10.2. Functions of local government in England

Counties	Districts
Education	Local planning and development control
Personal social services	Housing
Transportation	Local roads
Strategic planning	Environmental health
Fire services	Waste collection
Consumer protection	Local economic development (shared)
Waste disposal	Recreation and culture (shared)
Libraries	
Local economic development (shared)	
Recreation and culture (shared)	

Certain important functions commonly assigned to local government are not local government functions in England: health (a central government function, deconcentrated through the National Health Service); social welfare payments (handled by the central government's Benefits Agency); utilities such as water, sewerage, electricity, gas and telecommunications (all now privatised companies).

The police service, which was formerly a local government function (except in London), is now the responsibility of regional police authorities, which consist of representatives of both central and local government.

Over the last 20 years, there has been something of an erosion of the powers of local government. Important functions have been taken away from them: water supply (removed in the 1970s); further education colleges; and police (now jointly managed with central government). Much of the responsibility for education has been devolved to individual schools. The role of local governments in housing has also been much reduced as local governments have been required to sell the housing stock to tenants, while new social housing has been built mainly by independent housing associations. Increased central regulation has reduced the room for local discretion in the delivery of local services. Many other public agencies (sometimes known as quangos) are involved in areas that were formerly the domain of local government. On the other hand, local governments have been given increased responsibilities in the area of social services, and widened powers to address the well-being of residents. Increasingly, local governments are working in partnership with other public and private sector agencies, often providing leadership for such partnerships.

Financing Local Government

Organisation of local governments

Local councils are made up of representatives elected on a ward basis. The electoral term is four years. Elections are on a first-past-the-post basis. The three main political parties (Conservative, Labour and Liberal Democrat) occupy almost all the seats in local government, although there are a few minority parties and some independents. Control of the council goes to the largest party, but if that party does not have an overall majority, it has to establish a coalition with another party. A particular concern is the low voter turn-out in local elections – typically 30–45 per cent.

In most councils, political power resides with the leader of the largest party, who is one of the elected councillors. The leader selects the members of the Cabinet from among the elected councillors (subject to approval by the full council). The Cabinet has executive power and each Cabinet member has a portfolio, which generally corresponds to one (or more) of the main service departments. The remaining members of the Council serve on scrutiny committees, which examine the work of the executive. (The previous system of executive committees of councillors has been abolished in all but the smallest councils.) In this system the mayor (or lord mayor in a city) has no executive power but only a ceremonial role, including chairing the full council meeting.

A few councils (notably the GLA) have a directly elected mayor, rather than a leader. (The choice of whether or not to have an elected mayor is made through a referendum of all voters in the local government area.) The executive is then made up of the mayor plus a Cabinet drawn from the elected councillors, with other councillors serving on scrutiny committees.

Although national legislation does not specify the internal structure of local government, the management structure is remarkably uniform across the country. It is headed (in most cases) by a chief executive, who is a local government employee. There is a tradition of strong professional departments in English local government. The heads of these departments (usually one department for each of the main functional responsibilities) make up a management team of officers, chaired by the chief executive. All local government staff are directly employed by the local government; central government has no role in the appointment of staff.

Local government finance

Local governments account for around a quarter of total public spending in England. The largest areas of expenditure are education (36 per cent of gross local government spending), social services (16 per cent) and housing (14 per cent). County councils have much larger budgets than district councils, since they are responsible for the two largest services, education and social services.

Local governments have only one local tax, the council tax. This is a tax per household, which varies according to the value of the property occupied. Before 1990, local governments levied a property tax on all properties in their jurisdiction. Between 1990 and 1994, this was replaced by the community charge, a flat-rate poll tax on all citizens, with a few exceptions. Due to the unpopularity of the tax (and administrative problems), it was abandoned. It was replaced with the council tax, which is something of a hybrid between a poll tax and a property tax.

The council tax

The council tax is levied according to eight bands. The local government sets the annual tax rate for a band D property. The amount of tax payable is then determined by the band of property occupied, with the proportion of the band D tax that is applied being determined by the ratios set by legislation (see Table 10.3).

Table 10.3. Council tax property bands

	Capital value	Tax as percentage of band D
A	Up to £40,000	67
B	£40,000–52,000	78
C	£52,000–68,000	89
D	£68,000–88,000	100
E	£88,000–120,000	122
F	£120,000–260,000	144
G	£260,000–320,000	167
H	Over £320,000	200

The initial property valuation was done by the central government and was contracted out to local estate agents, who undertook it on a rapid assessment basis. The valuations have not been updated since 1993. The tax rate is set by the local government, although the central government sets a ceiling on annual increases (currently 5 per cent). There are reductions for single person households, and subsidies (council tax benefit) are available for those on low incomes.

The tax is collected by the local governments. In the case of two tier authorities, the tax is collected by the districts, including the part levied by the county. Most people pay through the banking system (direct debit), but other methods are available. Local governments have rigorous enforcement arrangements, with the power (obtained through the courts) to levy fines, attach earnings (i.e. obtain payment directly from employers), seize property and, ultimately, send non-payers to prison. The average collection rate (effectiveness) is around 95 per cent and the collection cost is around 0.5 per cent.

The tax has a number of problems:

• It is levied on the household, so that if the household moves without paying, the local government has to pursue them, since there is no liability on the landlord and any debt cannot be made a charge on the property; as a result, the collection rate is lower (95 per cent) than for the former property tax (but higher than for the poll tax).

- The tax is regressive, since the tax rate is much higher on low value properties than on high value properties.

- The tax is only levied on residential properties – business properties are subject to a separate central government tax (see below).

- Local governments have only one local tax – with grants accounting for two-thirds of their revenue, and the gearing effect is very high (a 5 per cent increase in expenditure necessitates a 15 per cent increase in council tax).

The council tax provides approximately 16 per cent of local governments' gross recurrent revenues. Fees, charges and rents provide a further 11 per cent. Most of the rest comes from central government revenue shares. Thus, local governments control less than 30 per cent of their resources, and most of those are subject to tight restrictions, for example of the level of charges for services and increases in council tax. In practice, local governments' room for manoeuvre over their total revenues is at most only 2–3 per cent.

Table 10.4. Local government revenue sources

Tax	Share of total recurrent revenue (%)
Council tax	16
Fees charges and rents	11
Business rates	13
Revenue support grant	21
Specific grants	29
Other	10

Central transfers

The business rate, a tax on business properties, is a central government tax which is shared 100 per cent with local government. (Until 1990, it was part of the local government's property tax.) It is collected by local government on behalf of the centre. The revenue is pooled and then redistributed on a per capita basis. Local governments can use it to meet their general expenditures.

The revenue support grant (or formula grant) is a block grant to local governments to meet their operating costs, including debt servicing. It is designed to provide all local governments with an equitable share of grant resources, taking account of relative expenditure needs and relative resource capacity. Expenditure needs are calculated using the 'formula spending assessment', which incorporates a large number of factors that are weighted (using regression analysis) to reflect their relative importance in determining local expenditure needs. Local government resource capacity is based on the amount that a local government could derive from the council tax if it levied it at a 'standard' rate. Since central government assesses the value of property for the council tax, it has complete information on the local tax base and hence on the amount of revenue which a local government could generate from the tax. Thus, the revenue support grant can be made fully equalising.

The specific grants include a number of different grants, some of which relate to the costs of specific services, particularly where the government is seeking to influence local government spending patterns towards particular activities. It also includes reimbursement of certain social welfare benefits that are administered by the local governments, such as housing benefit and council tax benefit.

Capital finance

Capital expenditure in England accounts for around 10 per cent of total expenditure. Housing and transport are the main areas of capital expenditure.

Traditionally, local governments in the UK financed most capital from borrowing. This is based on the benefit principle of equity that, since the benefits of capital expenditure accrue over many years, future generations should bear some of the costs of the expenditure by servicing the debt. More recently, a large proportion of capital expenditure has been met from capital receipts, particularly from the sale of local government housing stock, as well as other surplus property. In addition, there may be grants for certain forms of capital expenditure. Some capital assets, such as vehicles, are financed through leasing from private suppliers.

Borrowing may be from any source, including overseas, or from other local governments (there is an active market between local governments for short-term surplus funds). However, in practice, long-term borrowing is mainly from the Public Works Loans Board (PWLB), a central government agency that borrows money through government bonds. Although there is no subsidy element, the PWLB's terms are (marginally) more advantageous than other sources, so that in most cases there is no incentive for local governments to borrow elsewhere. The typical borrowing period is 25–30 years.

Borrowing was tightly controlled by the centre until recently, for reasons of macroeconomic management. However, since 2000 local governments have been responsible for controlling their own borrowing, in accordance with 'prudential rules' laid down by central government in association with the Chartered Institute of Public Finance and Accountancy (CIPFA), the professional body of local government finance officers.

Increasingly, public sector investment, including that by local governments, is undertaken through private finance initiative (PFI) schemes. These involve the private sector in building and managing the new capital asset (e.g. a school), with the local government leasing the facility from the private company. This avoids the need for the local government to borrow (and, in theory, brings private sector efficiency to the construction and management of the asset), but the cost implications for the local government may be the same as servicing a loan over time – and indeed there is plenty of evidence that the total costs may be higher.

Budgeting and financial management

The Director of Finance (or Treasurer or Chief Finance Officer) has responsibility for budgeting, financial management and accounting. S/he must be a qualified accountant. S/he has a statutory responsibility to report to central government any unlawful expenditures or decisions by the local government.

The annual budget process typically starts nearly a year before the budget year begins. The annual budget will be based on broader plans and strategies, such as the corporate vision and the medium-term economic and financial plan. These, together with central government policy statements about annual grant allocations, will determine the priority areas and the broad allocations of resources between sectors and services. Departmental heads and service managers will then be given budget ceilings and guidelines to work to in preparing their budgets. These departmental and service budgets are then aggregated. The gap between total budgeted expenditure and total income from fees and charges, revenue shares, grants (rate support grant plus specific grants) and any other sources will determine the level at which the council tax needs to be set to ensure a balanced budget. Balancing can be done from reserves and adjustments to departmental and service expenditure budgets, but the budget must balance (a legal requirement).

The final adjustments to the budget are often only agreed at the final meeting of the council (especially where one party does not have overall control).The budget has to be approved by the full council by 1 March, for the financial year that starts on 1 April. This allows time for council tax bills to be issued during March. There is no process of central government approval, although if a local government proposed to its increase council tax above the ceiling, it would be subject to central government intervention.

The capital budget is prepared alongside the recurrent budget, but is usually based on a three-year rolling capital programme. Debt servicing on borrowing is included within the recurrent budget.

Much of the responsibility for financial management is devolved to budget centres, such as departments or services, including individual schools. Central services provided to these budget centres, such as accounting or payroll services, are charged by the unit providing the service on the basis of a service-level agreement.

Auditing

Local governments have internal auditors whose main role is to ensure that systems are secure and not open to fraud. They may also carry out certain value for money exercises. External audit (ex-post) is conducted by the Audit Commission, using either in-house staff or private firms. External audit reports are placed before the council for action to be taken. In the past, external auditors could directly impose surcharges on officers or councillors deemed to have incurred losses, but that power is now exercised through the courts. Cases of fraud are referred to the police. Cases of corruption are rare, but not unknown. They are rare not only because there are effective systems in place to prevent fraud, but also because local government staff are generally well paid, and so are unwilling to jeopardise a safe and well-paid job for the risks involved in corruption. Increasingly, audit is concerned with efficiency and value for money, rather than just probity and fraud.

Most senior finance staff are members of CIPFA. Successful prosecution for fraud would mean that the person concerned would lose their membership and so be unable to work again as an accountant.

Note

1   This chapter deals only with local government in England; the systems in Scotland, Wales and Northern Ireland are all slightly different.

Further reading

Game, C. and Wilson, D. (2006). *Local Government in the United Kingdom*. Basingstoke: Palgrave-Macmillan.

Chandler, J. A. (2007). *Explaining Local Government: Local Government in Britain since 1800*. Manchester: Manchester University Press.

CHAPTER ELEVEN

The Dynamics of Fiscal Decentralisation: The Case of Ghana

Roger Oppong Koranteng

The aim of this case study is to understand the dynamics of the implementation of fiscal decentralisation in Ghana. In 1992 Ghana returned to civilian rule. A review of the Local Government Law of 1988 became necessary to bring it into compliance with the local government provisions contained in the constitution. Law 207 of the Provisional National Defence Council was therefore repealed by the promulgation of the Local Government Act, 1993. The implementation of the new decentralisation policy generated deep-seated political tension right from the outset, involving two interested parties who influenced local government law at the highest level of government.

This case study is based on research that used semi-structured interviews, documentary analysis and focus group discussions. More than 50 people were interviewed, including staff and consultants from the decentralisation secretariat, senior civil servants, academics, donors, representatives of the National Association of Local Government Authorities of Ghana (NALAG), former and present district chief executives of district assemblies and assembly members (councillors).

Responses and resistance to fiscal decentralisation

Distribution of the benefits

Fiscal decentralisation under the district assemblies' common fund (DACF) in Ghana is supposed to transfer more financial resources from the centre to the districts, and to provide fiscal autonomy for the district assemblies (Ayee, 2000). The district assemblies face two major structural challenges in relation to the implementation of fiscal decentralisation. Firstly, the DACF works out at an average of 15 per cent of the overall resource flows to the districts, in relation to funds for investment, whereas 85 per cent of financial resource flows are controlled by the central government institutions in the districts (MLGRD/GTZ, 2005). Secondly, approximately 90 per cent of staff operating at district level are on the payroll of central government agencies (MLGRD/DS, 2005). This situation has created tension between central government institutions and the district assemblies.

The central government agencies have argued that the district assemblies do not have capacity to take on bigger budget management responsibilities; this is rebutted by the district assemblies, which argue that they cannot prove their capacity if they do not receive resources with which to operate. This has resulted in deadlock. These inter-governmental tensions continue to characterise the implementation of fiscal decentral-isation in Ghana.

District assembly members argued, in interviews undertaken for this chapter, that cen-tral government agencies' resistance to fiscal decentralisation was a ploy to hold on to resources that should be transferred for greater and faster development. They chal-lenged the argument that capacities were not well established at the local level. In focus group discussions in Tema Municipality and East Akim (the two district assem-blies used as case studies), participants noted that the more resources they received, the more their capacities would develop. It was evident that the district assemblies had hardly any influence on the allocation of sector grants to their districts, and quite often did not have an administrative overview of the total resources flowing into their dis-tricts. Research indicated that significant amounts of off-budget fiscal resources were channelled into the districts by donors, thus escaping any district assembly administra-tive control (MLGRD/DS, 2005). Thus, fiscal decentralisation, which basically looks at revenue allocations commensurate with assigned responsibilities, with the aim of making districts financially viable and able to deliver services, has eluded the district assemblies.

It emerged from the focus group discussions that it was anomalous that district assem-blies were responsible for development and service delivery in all areas under their con-trol, but that sector departments working at the district level operate their budgets independently of the assemblies. It is important to note that some ministries, such as the Ministry of Health, have devolved an increasing proportion of their budgets to the regional and district offices, but these remain outside district assembly control. The assemblies argued that it was time for the government to see fiscal decentralisation as a major part of the solution to Ghana's developmental problems. They suggested that sector ministries should be put under pressure to disaggregate their budgets to form the basis of national budgetary allocations to government ministries, departments and agencies, and to the district assemblies.

Distribution of the cost of fiscal decentralisation

Implementation of fiscal decentralisation implies the loss of power, influence and con-trol over resources by sector ministries, including transferring finance for the salaries of field personnel from the centre to local government. More importantly, the Ministry of Finance and Economic Planning (MFEP), which perceived itself as bearing most of the impact and costs of fiscal decentralisation, resisted it. The ministry argues that decen-tralisation would give unrestrained spending power to the district assemblies and that this would interfere with the structural adjustment programmes (SAPs) which it is implementing. The SAPs, therefore, have provided an excuse for the lack of progress on fiscal decentralisation. It is evident that the reason for this failure is the reluctance of central government agencies, particularly the MFEP, to relinquish control of financial resources. There has been very little interest within the MFEP and other sector ministries in undertaking fiscal decentralisation and it is felt that the Ministry of Local Government and Rural Development (MLGRD) may not be strong enough to push for something so far-reaching. It is apparent that the cost in terms of loss of fiscal resources and power is focused on the central government agencies (Table 11.1). They will lose control over staff and finance if fiscal decentralisation is implemented.

Table 11.1. Fiscal decentralisation: arena of response and resistance

Characteristics of policy	Fiscal decentralisation
Dispersal of cost	Costs focus on central government institutions, which cede control of resources
Dispersal of benefits	Benefits are focused on sub-national levels of government, which are the recipients of resources
Technical and administrative complexity	Policy is functionally and technically complex, e.g. design of a formula for allocating resources
Level of public participation	Policy attracts limited public involvement – not visible to the public
Visibility of policy process	Policy requires sustained effort with few immediate visible returns

Source: Focus group discussions and interviews

Technical and administrative complexity and participation

In Ghana, political decentralisation has made more advances than administrative and fiscal decentralisation, probably because changes in political structures suited the politicians better than the other two forms of decentralisation. The Constitution and the Local Government Acts have provided an enabling environment for the implementation of fiscal decentralisation. However, the problem has been that there is a gap between the legal constitutional provision and actual practice. There was a consensus among the interviewees that the implementation of fiscal decentralisation was complicated and that it was the least understood aspect of decentralisation. It therefore involves considerable analytical work on a sector-by-sector basis, because what is applicable in one sector does not necessarily make sense in another. For example, the level of fiscal decentralisation in the agricultural sector may not make sense in health or education; sectoral differences may call for variations in the degree to which functions are decentralised. The exact division of roles and responsibilities between district assemblies and central government must be decided on a sector-by-sector basis.

Furthermore, the complexity of fiscal decentralisation means there must be an appropriate formula for sharing fiscal resources among the district assemblies and that the centre must develop the capacity to monitor and audit them. The implementation of fiscal decentralisation is technically and administratively complex; it needs careful analysis and sharing of functions among various levels of government (Prud'homme, 2003: 23). It therefore requires a high degree of sustained technical competence and commitment on the part of central government agencies. A structural challenge is the weak local revenue mobilisation at district level. To an overwhelming extent (85 per cent), the district assemblies are dependent on transfers from central government, both discretionary and conditional.

It also became evident from interviews with district level officers that the internally generated revenue mobilised by the district assemblies was basically used for paying sitting allowances to assembly members (councillors), and was not used for service delivery. The role of the public in the implementation of fiscal decentralisation has therefore been very limited. Because the district assemblies receive fiscal transfers from central government and have become dependent on them, there has been no motivation for them to look internally for alternative ways of generating revenue. This is supported by Olowu (2003), who argues that transfers are the predominant source of local government finance in Africa.

Visibility of the fiscal decentralisation policy process

The Ministry of Local Government and Rural Development issues guidelines in accordance with the Local Government Act (Act 462) and the District Assemblies Common Fund Act (Act 455) on the allocation of the DACF and its utilisation by the district assemblies. A broad disbursement of the DACF allocates 10 per cent of the fund as a 'reserve fund' retained at national level and 90 per cent to be shared among the district assemblies according to a formula approved by Parliament (Nicol, 2005). Half of this reserve fund is allocated to parliamentary constituencies managed by Members of Parliament for undertaking development projects, as a way of addressing the growing pressures on MPs to be directly involved in the development of their constituencies. Evidence from interviews with assembly members in the districts covered by the case study indicated that although district assembly members were unhappy about the modalities for the use of the proceeds of the DACF, its establishment has undoubtedly given district assemblies more credibility in their communities. However, it was evident that ordinary citizens could not distinguish between DACF projects and projects funded by other sources, such as donors. Furthermore, most members of the public viewed projects commissioned by their MP, funded by the parliamentary constituencies' share of the DACF and managed by the MP, as funded by money that came directly from the MP's pocket. This indicates that the implementation process of fiscal decentralisation is obscure and not fully understood by the public.

Actors' characteristics and fiscal decentralisation

This section applies a framework delineating the characteristics of the various stakeholders and their attitudes to fiscal decentralisation in order to make an empirical analysis of how they have influenced its implementation. The analysis identifies to what extent the different stakeholders have supported or constrained reform. The key actors include the MFEP, Members of Parliament, sector ministries, district assemblies, the MLGRD, the DACF administrator and donors. Table 11.2 summarises their stakes, level of interest, resources, capacity for mobilisation and attitudes towards fiscal decentralisation.

Table 11.2. Stakeholders' influence on fiscal decentralisation

Stakeholder	Stake	Interest in legislation	Resources available	Resource mobilisation capacity	Position
MFEP	Macroeconomic stability and fiscal discipline	Low	Financial, organisational and legitimacy	High	Opposition Negative
Members of Parliament	MPs' share in DACF	Medium	Constitutional, legal and legitimacy	High	Latent Positive
Sector ministries	Control over sectoral fiscal resources	Low	Information, organisation and legitimacy	High	Opposition Negative
District assemblies	Matching resources to implement transferred functions to districts	High	Constitutional, legal and legitimacy	Low	Promoters Positive
MLGRD	Centralisation and control over resources	Medium/ lukewarm	Technical, information and legitimacy	Medium	Promoter Positive
DACF administrator	Fair allocation of DACF to district assemblies	High	Constitutional, legal and legitimacy	High	Promoter Positive
Donors/ development partners	Strengthening decentralised units and overall capacity of district assemblies	High	External networks, financial and technical	High	Promoters Positive

Source: Focus group discussions and interviews

Ministry of Finance and Economic Planning: control freaks

The MFEP's key argument has been that the district assemblies do not have the capacity to manage financial resources. This argument was challenged in the Tema Municipality and East Akim District Assembly focus group discussions. Both groups argued that district assemblies were accountable, and that as representatives of the people involved in the budget and planning process, no matter how modest it might be, they knew that elements of accountability existed in the district assemblies. They debunked the capacity argument – that it was only after the district assemblies had been given the needed resources that they would be empowered and their capacity improved. In the process of decentralisation the axiom is: 'We decentralise to build capacity, and we build capacity to decentralise'. The question is: which comes first?

Members of Parliament: influential but latent

In fulfilment of its constitutional responsibilities, Parliament allocated 5 per cent of the total national revenue to the DACF; this has been transferred to the district assemblies annually since 1994. However in 2004, Parliament approved an increase in the proportion of total national revenue allocated to the DACF from 5 to 7½ per cent.

In the focus group discussions in both districts, the MPs' share of the common fund was called into question. It was argued that this sent wrong signals to the electorate that MPs should be the focus of development in their districts, rather than the district assemblies (councils). Focus groups observed that in the past MPs had been expected to bring development projects to their communities, but that now, as legislators, they should have nothing to do with the implementation of projects. It was further argued that MPs should not lose sight of their supervisory and oversight roles, and that they should avoid situations where they would have a conflict of interest and compromise their position.

From the above analysis, the stake of MPs in fiscal decentralisation is seen to be an increase in their share of the DACF, with only medium or less than maximum interest in the overall process. With their constitutional and legal resources, and high capacity for mobilisation, they could have influenced the effective implementation of the changes. Their position on fiscal decentralisation was positive, but they have not been active in pushing for reform.

Sector ministries: bureaucratic obscurantists

The sector ministries argue that because Ghana has 138 district assemblies, 1,306 zonal, urban, town and area councils, and 16,000 committee sub-structures (MLGRD, 2005), it is not financially or economically viable to decentralise fiscal resources. In other words, there is an economy of scale argument against fiscal decentralisation. Fjeldstad (2001) observed that fiscal decentralisation could increase the scope for corruption because in dispersing expenditure functions over a large number of units, controls would become increasingly ineffective. However, this argument was challenged by district assembly officials who pointed out that corruption at the local level is nothing compared to what happens at the centre. It was therefore evident that the sector ministries' stake in the issue of fiscal decentralisation was to maintain centralisation and control of fiscal resources, and that they preferred deconcentration of resources to their field offices. Their interest in fiscal decentralisation was low, and using their information, organisation and legitimate resources they mobilised strong opposition to its implementation. Their position on the whole issue was very negative, as shown in Table 11.2.

District assemblies: generals without armies

The interviews with district assembly members in both districts highlighted a number of arguments in favour of decentralisation. There was the welfare economics argument, which suggests that local decision-making in relation to expenditure functions is more efficient than central control, and that local decision-makers respond better than those at the centre to local needs. So district assemblies are in a better position to deliver services. There was also an accountability argument to the effect that district assemblies, as the highest political body at the district level, have a huge planning and budgeting responsibility. It was argued that with their elected councillors, district assemblies were more accountable to their communities than central government agencies, which had no local accountability. However, it was evident that most services were not delivered by the district assemblies. Services delivered by the sector departments, which are not necessarily accountable to local people, raise the issue of accountability. The assembly members further argued that the inability to integrate the decentralised departments into the district assemblies system had created difficulties for fiscal decentralisation in terms of integrating sectoral resources into the district assemblies.

From the above analysis, it is evident that the interest of district assemblies in fiscal decentralisation is to secure resources that match the functions that have been transferred to the districts. They have a substantial interest in the process, and possess constitutional and legal credibility. Although the assemblies have a low capacity for mobilisation because of their inadequate resources, their position on the issue was positive and they were promoters of decentralisation.

MLGRD: support for centralisation

The MLGRD, as the local government secretariat, is the supervisory ministry and is responsible for the planning, programming, monitoring and evaluation of policies affecting the district assemblies. In addition, it issues annual guidelines on the use of the DACF. The ministry has been authorised by the Local Government Act to exercise the following controls over the district assemblies, aimed at ensuring financial accountability:

- Issuing financial instructions;

- Issuing written instructions for better control and efficient management of the district assemblies' finances, after consultation with the Minister of Finance;

- Establishing an inspectorate division.

It was evident from the interviews with officials both within and outside the MLGRD that the ministry has centralising tendencies. Its infrastructural responsibility at the sub-national level makes the MLGRD responsible for some infrastructural investments in the districts. Its interest in centralisation stems from the fact that it controls a significant amount of infrastructure and investment money, which it is reluctant to relinquish. It was therefore in the MLGRD's interests to promote centralisation and central control of resources. The ministry had a medium interest in the process and possessed information and technical resources, with medium or less than adequate mobilisation capacity, as shown in Table 11.2. The MLGRD's position on fiscal decentralisation was lukewarm, even though it has been given a mandate to promote it.

The District Assemblies Common Fund Administrator

The DACF Administrator is by law appointed by the President of Ghana, with the approval of Parliament.

Interviews with the DACF Administrator indicated that his basic approach to sharing out the Fund was influenced by various factors, including need, service pressure, and the need to be responsive and to move towards greater equalisation.

- The need factor seeks to address the imbalance in the various levels of development among the district assemblies;

- The service pressure factor is determined by population density and pressure on the district's facilities;

- The need to be responsive motivates the district assemblies to mobilise more resources locally for development, instead of relying solely on the DACF

- There is pressure to ensure that each district, irrespective of size, natural endowment and population, is given an equal specified minimum for development.

The Administrator explained that the need factor was scored inversely, i.e. the fewer basic facilities a district possessed, the greater the score. Some of the facilities taken into account were the availability of health care (measured by patient/doctor ratio), education, water (taking into account quality and potability) and roads (the extent of tarred roads in a district, compared to the national situation). The service pressure factor could favour urban areas because it was based on land area in relation to population pressure and the responsibilities of local authorities. All the information was fed into a computer and proportional allocations were produced automatically.

What emerged from the focus group discussions in both districts were concerns about transparency in relation to the disbursement of the DACF within the areas covered by the district assemblies. The focus groups called for equitable distribution of the DACF among the various electoral areas within the districts and suggested the establishment of units in the district assemblies to monitor the DACF.

Donors and development partners

It became evident from interviews with local government officers that although donor-assisted programmes are well intentioned, many of them have been implemented through various sector ministries, departments and agencies. Donors make use of structures and approaches that are not always supportive of the fiscal decentralisation policy. For example, intra-sectoral consultation between donors and sector ministries have resulted in separate programmes for health, education and forestry at district level. These intra-sectoral donor co-ordination efforts have helped to shape and finance sectoral programmes in a deconcentrated manner, and in the process have made inter-sectoral co-ordination more difficult for the district assemblies. This problem is captured in the literature, which shows that donors have simultaneously supported decentralisation and favoured sector wide approaches (SWApS) that tend to recentralise power. Aid policies have frequently meant that donors support parallel administrative structures that in some cases have undermined the authority and capacity of elected local governments (Jütting et al., 2004).

Conclusion

This case study suggests that central government institutions, particularly the Ministry of Finance and Economic Planning, have resisted the implementation of fiscal decentralisation. District assemblies are perceived to be the main beneficiaries of the change. Fiscal decentralisation is technically and administratively difficult to implement when there is low public participation and visibility. It is apparent that reactions to fiscal decentralisation came from the bureaucratic arena, which had a lower political stake in its implementation.

Evidence based on stakeholder characteristics indicated that the key actors whose actions and resources constrained the implementation of the policy were, again, the central government agencies, led by the MFEP; the interest and resources of the district assemblies, on the other hand, were not significant enough to influence its implementation. In addition, it emerged that the MLGRD, with its centralising tendency, was not prepared to push for something as across-the-board as fiscal decentralisation, while donors were driving their own agendas, which sought to achieve sectoral programme objectives.

Fiscal decentralisation is designed to allow the district assemblies to gain access to national development resources for the implementation of development projects and programmes that have been prioritised in the district development plans. On the basis of the evidence provided in the preceding analysis, one can conclude that politics has operated to constrain policy-making on decentralisation and its implementation. The political attitudes of the key actors which accounted for the lack of achievement of fiscal decentralisation were a clear case of bureaucratic obscurantism, where the reluctance of bureaucrats at the centre to let go their hold on power and resources led to lack of progress in the reform. This also resulted in many unfulfilled mandates at district level, as district assemblies were not strong or resourceful enough to push for true fiscal decentralisation. In addition, the actions of donors, though well intentioned, did not always support the changes.

References

Ayee, J. (2000). *Decentralisation and Good Governance in Ghana*. Accra: Canadian High Commission.

Fjeldstad, O.-H. (2001). 'Intergovernmental Fiscal Relations in Developing Countries: A Review of Issues', Working Paper issue 11, pp. 1–15. Bergen, Norway: Chr. Michelsen Institute.

Fricker, P. (2005). *Local Governance – Poverty Reduction Support Programme*. Accra: MLGRD/GTZ.

Jütting, J. *et al.* (2004). 'Decentralisation and Poverty Reduction in Developing Countries: Exploring the Impact', Working Paper 236. Paris: OECD Development Centre, August, http://www.oecd.org/dataoecd/40/19/33648213.pdf

Ministry of Local Government and Rural Development (2005). *Financing Integrated Local Level Development: The Case of the District Budget*. Accra: MLGRD.

Ministry of Local Government and Rural Development/Decentralisation Secretariat (2005). *Phase 1 – Review of Local Government Investment Funding Practices (1999–2003) Final Report*. Accra: MLGRD.

Nicol, J.M. (2005). 'Financing Integrated Local Government Level Development: The District Assembly Common Fund', Paper presented at a workshop on Stakeholders Consultation with Parliamentary Committees of Finance and Local Government and Rural Development, 13–15 May 2005, Akosombo, Ghana.

Olowu, D. (2003). 'Local Institutional and Political Structures and Processes: Recent Experience in Africa', in Paul Collins (ed.), *Public Administration and Development: The International Journal of Management Research and Practice*, 23(1): 41–52.

Prud'homme, R. (2003). 'Fiscal Decentralisation in Africa: A Framework for Considering Reform', in Collins, P. (ed.), *Public Administration and Development: The International Journal of Management Research and Practice*, 23(1): 17–27.

CHAPTER TWELVE

Learning from Commonwealth Experience

Munawwar Alam

The Commonwealth Secretariat has developed an executive programme on finance for sub-national and local governments in collaboration with the School of Public Policy, University of Birmingham, UK. The programme affords participants an opportunity to highlight current practices in their countries and to share them with others. In order to facilitate in-depth analysis and review of local government financial systems, the programme requires the preparation of country papers. This chapter presents case studies from selected Commonwealth countries, and looks at current practices in local government, under the following headings:

1. External control of local finances by the central or state/provincial government ministry, e.g. approval of the budget, taxes, loans and constraints in the political, legal and policy contexts

2. Annual taxation capacity

3. Potential for improvements in revenue collection

4. Ratio of tax collection to taxes due

5. Revenue generated through charging for services

6. Central-local financial relations: the kind and extent of intergovernmental transfers and grants

7. Ability to access capital markets for investment resources

8. Bond flotations for capital investment

9. Local government audit mechanisms

*The author wishes to thank the following contributors and participants in the workshops for their valuable input: Amiruddin Bin Muhammed (Malaysia); Naudia Leonie Crosskill (Jamaica); Sarah Ann Lewis (Sierra Leone); Silvio Frendo (Malta); Sarwansingh Purmessur (Mauritius); Zaheda Begum Lall Mahomed (Mauritius); Chinedu Schola Brown (Nigeria); T.M.P. Tennakoon (Sri Lanka).

10. E-governance processes, e.g. for payment of taxes, dues, licensing, complaints, etc.

11. Transparency: how can budgeting can be made more open to public influence?

External control of local finances

In **Malaysia**, local council members are appointed by the state government and most of them are political appointees. The central government allocates operating and development expenditure to local governments through the state governments. Income from licensing, taxes and fines can be used by local governments for the benefit of their areas.

In **Jamaica**, the central government controls over 90 per cent of local finances. The financial framework within which the council operates is as follows:

• Parochial Revenue Fund

• Government grant

• Equalisation fund

• Self-financing

• General Revenue Fund

Local authorities prepare budgets, but these have to be approved by the Ministry of Local Government. Government grants and the Parochial Revenue Fund make up 89 per cent of local authority budgets, and local authorities have no control over these allocations. The Parochial Revenue Fund is comprised of property taxes and motor vehicle licence fees, and central government decides when these taxes can be increased and by how much. Disbursement of monies provided through loans is done through the Ministry of Local Government; local authorities are not involved in the loan process.

The sources of revenue over which local councils have control are the self-financing and general revenue sources. However, the development of these sources is constrained by political considerations, because tax increases can affect politicians at the polls. Local authorities are not involved in the policy decisions that affect them. However, this is gradually changing as they are realising that they need to be involved. In addition, the Jamaican Government has developed a consultation code which is intended to increase the influence of local people on policy decisions.

In **Sierra Leone**, local councils derive their authority from the Local Government Act of 2004. Section 20 of the Act confers the highest political authority on the locality, with legislative and executive powers. External control of local councils is therefore restricted to policy issues. In addition, Section 43 (2) of the Act makes local councils responsible for the preparation, administration and control of budgetary allocations in all their departments.

In **Malta**, the financial operations of local councils are regulated by the Local Councils Act and various regulations and procedures concerning finance, audit and tendering. Although each council is an autonomous body, the Department for Local Government monitors their operations to ensure that they operate within the legislation.

Local councils' main income comes from funds allocated by the central government according to a formula drawn up in the 10th Schedule of the Act. Each council is required to draw up an annual budget and a three-year business plan. These two documents are open to public scrutiny. Councils must also publish quarterly financial reports throughout the year, as well as an annual administrative report at the year-end

Local councils may not:

(i) Borrow or lend any monies except with the approval of the minister responsible for local government with the concurrence of the Minister of Finance. Each application is vetted by the Department for Local Government, which ensures that the council can sustain the repayments imposed by the loan and therefore will not negatively affect the operations of local councils;

(ii) Enter into any form of commercial partnership, unless authorised to do so in writing by the minister;

(iii) Delegate any of its functions in a manner other than that established by the Local Councils Act;

(iv) Donate any sums or make any donation in kind to any non-government organisation not included in Schedule Eight of the Local Councils Act. However, a council may give a donation of not more than Lm50 in one year to an organisation in the locality which is not listed in Schedule Eight. The total amount of donations in one year must not exceed 0.5 per cent of a Council's annual allocation.

The minister responsible for local government may require any document from a local council.

In **Mauritius**, the central government provides an annual grant-in-aid to all local authorities for their recurrent budget. An annual amount is also provided for capital expenditure.

According to Sections 105 and 107 of the Local Government Act, each local authority must submit an estimate of its income and expenditure for each financial year for approval by the Minister of Local Government. No expenditure can be incurred at the start of the financial year unless the approval of the minister has been obtained. The expenditure of a local authority during any year must not exceed the amount laid down in the approved estimate without the minister's approval.

In order to submit a balanced budget, the local authorities have to top up the amount obtained as grant-in-aid by raising revenue from other sources, namely, local rates (municipal taxes), trade licence fees and other charges for development and building permits. The amount of rates and other charges that can be imposed by local authorities does not require the approval of the Minister of Local Government.

Local authorities are also allowed to borrow money from financial institutions; very often, these loans are guaranteed by the central government.

In **Nigeria**, the state gives only technical advice through the Ministry of Local Government. This is done through monthly meetings of the joint accounts allocation committee, which is made up of the chairs of the 17 councils and senior staff from the ministry. The legislative arm of each council approves the budgets, loans, taxes and rates on their legislative list.

In **Sri Lanka**, the central government and provincial councils have no formal control over local authority finance. Local authorities prepare their budgets, which must be approved by the local council. A grant for reimbursement of some special payments is released by the provincial council with money received from central government. This grant is used for the following local government payments:

- Staff salaries

- Allowances of council members

- Revenue aids for low-income local governments.

The provincial council releases grants to the local authorities through the Department of Local Government, which is a provincial council department, operating under a commissioner.

Annual taxation capacity

In **Malaysia**, the annual taxation capacity of a medium-sized local government is approximately RM100–150 million. This amount is enough for a local authority to be self-funding. Large and small local authorities sometimes need financial assistance from the Federal Government in the form of grants.

In **Jamaica**, the local authorities' taxation capacity is low. They are involved in the collection of property taxes and trade licences, but only to a limited extent. Ultimately, taxable capacity is determined by the economic state of the parish.

In **Malta**, local councils are not empowered to collect taxes. At present they obtain their main income from central government. They also receive money derived from the payment of fines in their locality, and a very small amount comes from organising activities such as lectures and courses. The revenue figures for the financial year 2004–2005 were:

Government allocation: Lm10.6m

Income from other sources: Lm2.6m.

In **Mauritius**, local authorities are divided into two types: one for urban areas, i.e. municipal councils; and one for rural areas, i.e. district councils. The law provides that municipal councils can charge a local rate on immovable properties. This is calculated as a percentage of the net annual rental value of properties found within the administrative boundary of each municipal council. The district councils are also allowed to charge such rates, but this is subject to the prior approval of the President of the Republic. As yet, no district council has charged any local rate.

In **Nigeria**, it is difficult to generalise, as annual taxation capacity varies from one local government to another. It is quite low in rural local governments, but larger in urban authorities.

In **Sri Lanka**, local governments are empowered to collect some taxes from the local community under the Local Government Act. The following are the main sources of taxation:

- Rates and taxes from local residents

- Licences for meat stalls

- Other trading licences

- Exhibitions, advertising banners and boards

- Entertainment (cinema, concerts, etc.)

- Charges for bus stands and car parks

- Taxes on new housing plans

- Taxes on bicycles, carts and taxies

- Garbage tax

Potential for improvements in revenue collection

It was suggested that in **Malaysia** there is a need to strengthen the enforcement team to generate more revenue and at the same time introduce more facilities and services for the public. In addition, local government should educate the public so that they meet their obligations.

The following recommendations were made in relation to **Jamaica**:

- Engage in discussion with all key stakeholders;

- Re-examine policies and administrative procedures for enhancing local revenues;

- Improve enforcement capabilities;

- Mobilise political will;

- Improve service delivery;

- Engage taxpayers in the process so that they can understand the rationale for the mobilisation;

- Motivate management and operational staff to become integrally involved in the process;

- Ensure that management follows all the regulations and procedures to ensure transparency and credibility of the process.

In **Sierra Leone**, because of political and legal constraints, the substantial revenue potential of councils is not realised. The National Revenue Authority, which is the main revenue arm of central government, has overall authority.

The core revenue streams of the city council of Freetown (the country's capital) are:

- Property rates

- Market dues

- Fees and licences.

There is lack of proper co-ordination between central and local government in the areas of property registration and issuing building permits, and this is hampering the city council from realising its full potential. The responsibility for issuing building permits has not been transferred to the local council as one of its devolved functions. In fact, the central government owes huge rate arrears in respect of state properties. Less than 18 per cent of rates revenue in the municipality is actually collected, and the council would be able to collect a much higher proportion if the central government gave it active support. Local councils would then be much less reliant on central government subventions. Freetown city council has 32 councillors, four of whom are from the ruling party and 28 from the opposition. This situation has led to political problems in achieving financial autonomy.

It was suggested that better law enforcement by local wardens in **Malta** could increase local council revenues. Councils should also look at possible ways in which they could use existing facilities for council activities which would generate funds.

Some radical ideas were put forward in relation to **Mauritius**, for example:

- Local rates should be introduced in rural areas;

- Small business people, for example, market stallholders, should be charged a market rent for their stalls. These stalls could be allocated by open tender in order to obtain a better return;

- Many services, for example scavenging, could be carried out in-house instead of being contracted out, subject to this being cost-effective;

- Loans should be deployed as soon as they are borrowed;

- A culture of user payments should be fostered.

It was suggested that local authorities could reduce the cost of borrowing by mobilising funds through the issue of bonds.

In **Nigeria**, it was suggested that revenue mobilisation could be improved in the following ways:

- Making vehicles available for tax drives, because of the difficulty of securing voluntary compliance from taxpayers;

- Creating awareness in local councils of the need to collect revenue to fund development programmes;

- Providing people-oriented projects to enhance revenue generation and voluntary payment;

- There should be a serious effort to stop revenue leakages through tax collectors.

Revenue mobilisation in **Sri Lanka** could be improved through the implementation of legal procedures. Tax defaulters should be brought to book and castigated. Construction and other maintenance work, which is currently carried out by central government through contractors, could be handed over to local governments, which could make a profit by using their own machinery, equipment and labour.

Ratio of tax collection to taxes due

Table 12.1. Tax collection ratios

Country	Ratio	Remarks
Malaysia	5:1	This ratio is based on one medium-sized city council
Jamaica	35:65	
Malta		Local councils are not empowered to collect taxes
Mauritius	80 per cent	
Nigeria	*Rural:* 42.6 per cent	
	Semi-urban: 28.5 per cent	
	Urban: 36.26 per cent	
Sri Lanka	80 per cent	

Revenue generated through charging for services

In **Malaysia**, the revenue generated depends on the size of local government, e.g. Kuala Lumpur City Council (the biggest city council in Malaysia) generates about RM100 million a year from service charges. The main challenge is to ensure that the services are efficient and delivered on time.

In *Jamaica*, only 8 per cent of revenue comes from service charges. The services are:

- Building inspection
- Barbers' and hairdressers' licences
- Butchers' licences
- Places of amusement
- Fees for burial inspection
- Charges for billboards and signs
- Trade licences.

In *Malta*, very little revenue is generated through charging for services. Such revenue comes mainly from the organisation of lectures and courses, and advertisements on property owned by local councils. Only 1.4 per cent of local councils' total income is generated by service charges.

Any income generated by a local council has to be covered by by-laws. Such by-laws must be approved by the minister responsible for local government.

In *Mauritius*, licence fees account for 40 per cent of the total revenue of local authorities. These include processing fees for development and building permits, and charges for market stalls and from buses for using traffic centres. As local authorities have a duty to ensure the well-being of their citizens, provided that such services are not considered as a revenue-generating activity, but rather as a way of bettering the living conditions of their citizens, these fees are generally acceptable.

In *Nigeria*, service revenue are small. Charges include antenatal fees, fees for approval of building plans, identification charges and property rates (for urban councils only). People are unwilling to pay because the services are unsatisfactoy. There is also a lack of awareness of the availability or need for some of the services.

In *Sri Lanka*, 20 per cent of total local government income comes from services provided by local governments. These include:

- Piped water
- Waste collection
- Streetlights (no charges)
- Crematorium service
- Vaccination of dogs (no charges)
- Health services for children and pregnant mothers (no charges)

- Ambulance service

- Hearse service.

If charges are too high, local governments may face a problem. However, so far there are no reports of any objections.

Central-local financial relations

In **Malaysia**, the Federal Government allocates operating and development expenditure to local governments through state governments. All allocations are treated as grants and the local government can apply for soft loans from the Federal Treasury if necessary. Where services have been privatised centrally, the central government will allocate the amount as grant to assist the local government if performance falls below the threshold agreed in the privatisation agreement.

In **Jamaica**, central government provides monthly allocations in the form of:

- Government grant

- Motor vehicle licences

- Property taxes.

In **Malta**, local councils' main source of income is the annual allocation granted by central government. This is forwarded every quarter in advance and directly transferred to the councils' bank accounts.

In **Mauritius**, the central government provides an annual grant to local authorities for recurrent and capital expenditure. The recurrent expenditure grant accounts for 70 per cent of the total budget, while the grant for capital projects is mostly for minor schemes implemented by the local authorities. Other more substantial capital investments are financed from capital fund, surplus fund, loans or special grant. Consequently, projects may be wholly or partly financed by central government, or local authorities are allowed to borrow money from the financial institutions and the loans are guaranteed by the central government. For some projects, the central government repays the loan, while for others the local authorities have to repay it from their own funds.

In **Nigeria**, the financial relationship is determined by the decisions of the joint account allocation committee. Projects are occasionally jointly funded by the state and local government. Pay-as-you-earn tax, collected from local government employees, is paid over to the state internally-generated revenue fund. The state government is supposed to pay to the local councils 10 per cent of its total internally-generated revenue.

In **Sri Lanka**, the government releases money to local governments as grants.

Ability to access capital markets for investment resources

In *Malaysia*, the Local Government Act 1976 and Financial Procedure Act 1957 allow local governments to invest surplus funds on deposit in any bank, or in securities issued by the Federal Government or in trust funds issued by the Crown Agents, subject to the written approval of the Federal Treasury.

In *Jamaica*, local authorities are prohibited from accessing the capital market.

In *Sierra Leone*, the ability of local councils to access capital markets is restricted, because at present there is no financial capital market structure. However, there are opportunities for local councils to access venture capital through established finance houses by issuing municipal bonds in an effort to aggregate funding for major capital projects. This must be approved by the Ministry of Local Government and Community Development and the Ministry of Finance.

In *Malta*, local councils are only authorised to invest their money in government leased securities, including stocks, bonds and bills.

In *Mauritius*, local authorities are allowed to borrow money from the financial institutions. The loans are invariably guaranteed by central government, which assesses the local authority's ability to repay the loan before guaranteeing it.

In *Sri Lanka*, additional money can be deposited in a bank as fixed deposits. However, there is no opportunity to access capital markets.

Bond flotations for capital investment

In *Malaysia*, local governments can float bonds for viable projects, subject to the approval of the Federal Treasury. The bonds are guaranteed by the state government, which improves their rating.

This system is not practised in *Jamaica*; the law allows it, but the state of the local councils' affairs means that it is not practicable.

In *Sierra Leone*, local councils' ability to access capital markets is much restricted because at present there is no financial capital market structure. However, there are opportunities for local councils to access venture capital through established finance houses by issuing municipal bonds in an effort to aggregate funding for major capital projects. Ultimate approval rests with the Ministry of Local Government and Community Development and the Ministry of Finance.

Local government audit mechanisms

In *Malaysia*, local government accounts are monitored by the Ministry of Local Government to ensure financial probity. They are also audited by a representative of the Auditor-General on a routine basis and in the event of a complaint. Selected projects are subject to a management audit to ensure transparency and avoid fraud.

In *Jamaica*, the council's auditor first checks all vouchers and works as they arise. Two sets of external auditors visit all councils on an annual basis: one from the Ministry of Local Government and the other from the Auditor-General's department. The auditors from the Auditor-General's department are deemed more independent, since the local councils do not report to them, but to the Ministry.

In *Sierra Leone*, local councils are subject to internal and external periodic audit checks. The frequency of the external audit is determined by the Auditor-General: for the internal audit, random sampling is supposed to be undertaken every three months. The Chief Administrator receives a regular quarterly report from the internal auditor and this is a standing agenda item at meetings of the council.

Although councils have a degree of independence in the management of their budgets, they have to report to the Local Government Finance Department. The department reviews their budget and development plans before approving the release of government subventions for community development projects.

The department also ensures that local councils comply with financial control guidelines such as the Finance Administration Regulations (FAR) and the Comprehensive Local Government Performance Appraisal System (CLGPAS).

In *Malta*, the Auditor-General appoints local government auditors to audit the accounts of local councils and lays down the conditions under which they operate. Local government auditors are appointed for a year at a time, renewable each year, for a total period of not more than five consecutive years. Their remuneration and expenses are paid by the Auditor-General. They must submit reports to the Auditor-General not later than the end of June of each year, and copies of the reports are transmitted to the minister responsible for local government, the Director for Local Government and the respective local council. A copy must also be laid on the table of the House of Representatives by the Minister for Local Government within six weeks of its receipt.

Local government auditors must hold a warrant to act as an auditor issued under the Accountancy Profession Act, or be a duly registered partner in a firm of auditors.

In the exercise of their duties, local government auditors have access to all books, records, returns and other documents relating to the accounts of local councils and may require any person holding or accountable for any such documents to appear before them at the audit. In the case of a possible irregularity, abuse of control or fraud in the council's financial affairs, the minister may request an investigation to be conducted by the Auditor-General or by a board appointed under the Inquiries Act or by any other means he deems fit. If a councillor is found to have fraudulently made an illegal payment, they may be held personally liable and the Director for Local Government will take the necessary action for the recovery of the money.

All purchases between Lm500 and Lm2000 must be supported by three signed quotations or be committed through the issue of a public tender. Purchases costing over Lm2000 must be made through the issue of a public tender.

In **Mauritius**, each local authority has its own internal auditors who report to its chief executive if they find any anomaly. The final accounts are audited by the Department of the Director of Audit, a central government body. The audited accounts are then submitted to the Ministry of Local Government, which scrutinises the report and takes the local authority to task if the need arises.

In **Nigeria**, local government councils each have an internal audit department. the financial regulations and councils' activities are overseen by the Office of the Auditor-General within each state government and an inspectorate division within the Ministry of Local Government.

In **Sri Lanka**, the Auditor-General is responsible for making an independent audit of each local authority, under the Constitution. A separate audit branch of the Auditor-General's office operates in all town and municipal councils. In small councils (*pradeshia sabba*), the audit is carried out by a superintendent of audit who is entrusted with the work by the Auditor-General.

Internal audits are also carried out by the internal audit sections of municipal councils, as an internal control.

E-governance processes

The Government of **Malaysia** launched the Malaysian Public Sector ICT Strategic Plan in August 2003 to provide clear direction on the use of information and communication technology (ICT) for service delivery. Under this system payment of taxes, licensing, rental, fines and complaints can be channelled online.

In **Malta**, local councils are very heavily involved in e-governance.

- All 68 local councils provide free internet access to the public.

- All local councils have signed an agreement with central government by which they bind themselves to increase local e-government services; central government assigns public officials to work with local councils.

- In 2003, the MyWeb Project was launched, under which ICT awareness training was given to all interested members of the public.

- Local councils have an e-customer care system which has been in place since 2002; once a member of the public lodges a complaint at a local council, this is channelled to the respective government department/authority. Action is taken and the complainant is informed of the outcome.

- Local councils have an online system for the payment of fines, introduced in 2003, by which any member of the public can pay a fine electronically.

- Members of the public can also pay government rents through another online system.

In **Mauritius**, the municipalities and district councils are partly computerised, mainly in relation to the collection of taxes and dues. The Ministry of Local Government has launched a tender for the elaboration of an e-business plan for local authorities. This tender exercise is almost completed and the consultancy will be appointed shortly.

In **Jamaica** and **Nigeria**, local councils have not yet embarked on e-governance. The lack of a power supply to most councils and lack of staff capacity is a serious limitation in Nigeria.

In **Sri Lanka**, some local governments are introducing e-governance for their routing work. These schemes are still at pilot stage.

Transparency: how can budgeting can be made more open to public influence?

In relation to **Malaysia**, it was suggested that pre-budget dialogue could be organised between local governments and residents' associations, and that NGOs and public and private agencies should be included in the dialogue. Their suggestions and feedback would ensure that projects and services provided maximum benefit for all.

In **Jamaica**, the following measures were identified as ways of making the budgeting process more transparent and people-centred:

- Identify key stakeholder groups;

- State realistic and achievable budget targets;

- Ask stakeholders to state what they desire for their communities and parish;

- Utilise the consultation code.

In **Sierra Leone**, the budgets of local councils are set by a participatory process starting at ward committee and community level; during this process the developmental aspirations of the various communities are translated into development plans which are put before the council for its approval. However, the council approves its own budget, in accordance with guidelines from the Local Government Finance Department.

It was explained that in **Malta** there is a system under which the public is involved in setting the council budget. Before a local council considers its annual financial estimates, it holds a meeting that is open to everybody who is on the electoral register for the area. This meeting must be held at least once a year at a venue determined by the council and as far as possible the venue must be accessible to all, including wheelchair users. A notice advertising the meeting is published in all daily newspapers, and broadcast on all national radio stations.

The mayor, assisted by the executive secretary, ensures that the agenda for the annual meeting includes a report on the performance of the council during the previous year and the business plan for the following year.

The meeting is chaired by the mayor and the executive secretary keeps a record of the proceedings, including any complaints or suggestions. The minutes of the meeting are discussed by the council during its first meeting after the locality meeting. The council then follows up the complaints and suggestions as it sees fit.

A copy of the council's annual budget is open for public viewing at the council offices during normal office working hours. Most councils also publish their budget on their official website.

The public can attend all council meetings. Although members of the public are not allowed to participate, they can take notes of the proceedings and can then lodge a complaint or suggestion to the council through its customer care system.

In **Mauritius**, the budget of each local authority is prepared by its finance committee, which is made up of a number of councillors, assisted by the council's financial controller. If consultation seems appropriate, there is provision for discussions to be held with NGOs, pressure groups and other organisations. However, it was felt that consultation processes can send the wrong signal and build up people's hopes that projects will be carried out when in fact the funding for them is unavailable.

It was advocated that in **Nigeria**, the current community economic empowerment and development strategy should be strengthened so that the public can contribute to the preparation, presentation and debate on the budget before it reaches the legislative arm of the local government

In **Sri Lanka**, the budget is based on proposals from local government members, which incorporate the area's development needs and maintenance requirements. Members of the public are also able to submit proposals to council members as well as direct to the council.

Index

design issues 83–5
England 119–20
erosion of local effort 83
evaluation criteria 81–2
fiscal decentralisation 20
grants 79–82, 85–7
inherent tensions 83
objectives 77–8
overdependence on centre 83
revenue sources 23–4, 26
tax sharing 78
types 78–81
use of different types 84
investment *see* capital investment

Jamaica
audit mechanisms 143
bond flotations 142
capital markets access 142
central-local relations 141
control of finances 134
e-governance 145
service charges 140
taxation 136–9
transparency 145
joint ventures 58

Kenya 33–4
Koranteng, Roger Oppong 8, 123–32

leasing 58
leveraging 57–8
LGUGC (Local Government Unit
Guarantee Corporation), Philippines 63
licenses, business 31, 33–4
loans 52–3, 55–6, 80–1
Local Government Act 1972, England 114
Local Government Unit Guarantee
Corporation (LGUGC), Philippines 63

Malaysia
audit mechanisms 142–3
bond flotations 142
capital markets access 142
central-local relations 141
control of finances 134
e-governance 144
service charges 139
taxation 136–7, 139
transparency 145

Malta
audit mechanisms 143–4
capital markets access 142
central-local relations 141
control of finances 135
e-governance 144–5
service charges 140
taxation 136, 138–9
transparency 145–6
management accounting 101
Manor, J. 16
market access, Commonwealth 142
market development, Tamil Nadu 70–3
matching grants 80
Mauritius
audit mechanisms 144
capital markets access 142
central-local relations 141
control of finances 135–6
e-governance 145
service charges 140
taxation 137–9
transparency 146
mayors 117
MCIs (municipal credit institutions) 55–6
MDFs (municipal development funds) 55–6,
63, 70–1
medium-term expenditure framework
(MTEF) 89
Members of Parliament (MPs), Ghana 127–8
MFEP (Ministry of Finance and Economic
Planning), Ghana 124–5, 127–8, 131
Millennium Development Goals 11, 97–8
Ministry of Finance and Economic Planning
(MFEP), Ghana 124–5, 127–8, 131
Ministry of Local Government and Rural
Development (MLGRD) 125–31
monitoring budgets 102–3
MPs (Members of Parliament), Ghana 127–8
MTEF (medium-term expenditure frame
work) 89
municipal banks 62
municipal bonds 57, 61
municipal credit institutions (MCIs) 55–6
municipal development funds (MDFs) 55–6,
63, 70–1
municipal infrastructure 60–76
innovative approaches 60–76
international experiences 61–3
Tamil Nadu 63–73

skills
  decentralisation 15
  local lack 15, 98, 123–4, 128
  Tamil Nadu ULBs 72
sources of revenue 2–3, 23–40
  capital investment 50
  choices locally 37–8
  England 119
  lack of sources 15
  local sources 24–5
  money shortages 26
  the need 23–4
  property taxation 32, 34–7
  selecting sources 27–9
  service charges 38–40
  taxation 23–38
South Africa 62
specific grants 79–80, 82, 86, 119
Sri Lanka
  audit mechanisms 144
  capital markets access 142
  central-local relations 141
  control of finances 136
  e-governance 145
  service charges 140–1
  taxation 137, 139
  transparency 146
stability of economy 16
staff grants 79–80
structural adjustment programmes (SAPs)
  124–5
subsidies 39, 80–1
supply and demand, Tamil Nadu 70–3
surcharges on taxation 38
Sverrisson, A. 17
systems-based auditing 106

Tamil Nadu 4–5, 61, 63–73
  bond model diagram 71
  capital investment 64–5
  finance gaps 65
  market development 70–3
  MDF framework 70
  need for finances 63–5
  performance 68
  TNUDF 4, 65–8
  ULBs 63–73
  WSPF 68–70
Tamil Nadu Urban Development Fund
  (TNUDF) 4, 65–8

Tamil Nadu Urban Infrastructure Financial
  Services Limited (TNUIFSL) 65–8
targets 48
tariffs 43
taxation 23–38, 41–9
  business rate 119
  collection 27, 44, 47, 137–9
  Commonwealth 136–9
  council tax 117–19
  effectiveness 41–9
  efficiency 28, 42, 45–9
  identifying taxpayers 43–4, 46
  implementation 28
  Kenya 33–4
  local choices 37–8
  neutrality 28
  potential 42
  principal forms 29–32
  property 32, 34–7, 86
  raising awareness 48
  rates 38
  selection criteria 27–9
  sharing taxes 38, 78
  suitability 27–9
  surcharging taxes 38
  tax effort 41–2
  use of revenues 38
technical competence, Ghana 125–6
TNUDF (Tamil Nadu Urban Development
  Fund) 65–8
traditional auditing 105–6
transfers see intergovernmental transfers
transparency 145–6
trends, global 11–12
TSUIFSL (Tamil Nadu Urban Infrastructure
  Financial Services Limited) 65–8

UK see United Kingdom
ULBs (urban local bodies), Tamil Nadu 63–73
unavoidable costs 102
United Kingdom (UK) 104–7, 114–22
United States (US) 61–2, 70–1
unity, national 14
urban local bodies (ULBs), Tamil Nadu
  63–73
US see United States

valuation, property tax 36
Venkatachalam, Pritha 4, 60–76
virements 95

visibility issues, Ghana 126
Von Braun, J. 17

Water and Sanitation Pooled Fund (WSPF)
68–70
World Bank 66

WSPF (Water and Sanitation Pooled Fund)
68–70
yield, taxation 27

zero-based budgeting (ZBB) 93–4
Zimbabwe 62